Acclaim for John J. Tassone's

Go For It!

"I had the pleasure of reading *Go For It!* and found it very insightful. The book was easy to read and relate to even for a person who is not in the sales end of business."

— *Diane Steiner, FLMI, Vice President, Life Underwriting, Pekin Insurance Company*

"Having been in the insurance business for thirty-eight years, it is very easy to pick up on John Tassone's enthusiasm for helping people. The value of his advice is immeasurable. This should be a must-read for everyone entering the sales arena and the business world. It's the one book that covers all the basics needed to build a successful career, whether working for a large corporation or working in your own business. *Go For It!* is truly a practical guide to success."

— *Bob Trezek, CEO, Bob Trezek Insurance Services*

"John Tassone recharged my attitude toward my career as a health insurance agent. Sales were pretty good, and I had become a bit complacent. After reading *Go For It!*, I was able to believe in myself, set big goals, and think more positively. I recently received a promotion and am handling larger accounts. John's ideas have had a powerful influence on my career."

— *Nicole Dotson, Milwaukee, Wisconsin*

More Acclaim for
Go For It!

"A great how-to book for those who want to improve their sales skills — and sales results! John Tassone proves that success comes to anyone who's willing to work hard and apply some simple, commonsense, time-tested ideas."

> — *John Beniaris, CPCU, President,*
> *Midwest Security Services, Inc.*

"John's knowledge has helped me understand the insurance business and what makes people tick. *Go For It!* is not only an enjoyable read but also teaches valuable lessons in people skills and how to conduct yourself in the business environment."

> — *Jim Tram, CPCU, Sales Manager,*
> *Pekin Insurance Company*

Go
For It!

A Practical Guide to
Success for Everyone

John J. Tassone

Cypress House

GO FOR IT!
A Practical Guide to Success for Everyone
Copyright © 2011 by John J. Tassone

Cypress House
155 Cypress Street
Fort Bragg, CA 95437
(800) 773-7782
www.cypresshouse.com

Book and cover design: Michael Brechner / Cypress House

Cover photograph: Copyright © Mark Evans 2008 / iStockphoto

LIBRARY OF CONGRESS CATALOGING-IN-PUBLICATION DATA

Tassone, John J.
  Go for it! : a practical guide to success for everyone / John J. Tassone.
-- 1st ed.
    p. cm.
  ISBN 978-1-879384-81-1 (pbk. : alk. paper)
  1. Success in business. 2. Success. I. Title.
  HF5386.T235 2010
  650.1--dc22   2010042969

PRINTED IN THE USA

2 4 6 8 9 7 5 3 1

I dedicate this book to my wife Catherine,
who has always stood behind me
in everything I have done.

To my children,
Kathleen and Daniel,
my grandchildren,

and a special dedication
to my daughter Erica,
who passed away in June 2007.

Disclaimer

In the forty-four years that I have been selling insurance and been involved with the insurance industry, I have read numerous books and articles and attended many motivational meetings and seminars dealing with selling, believing in yourself, and positive thinking. Also, in the course of my travels in this industry, I have met hundreds of people from all walks of life, who would pass on tidbits of information, an anecdote, or some fact or story they may have come upon.

In *Go For It!*, I have mentioned dozens of these anecdotes, and mention tidbits of information I might have heard years ago. I wish to make it very clear that I do not claim originality or take credit for any of the sayings I mention in this book. The truth is I don't know where much of this information or the anecdotes originated. Over the years I have compiled an abundance of knowledge including hundreds of sayings and anecdotes, which I have drawn upon in writing this book, all of them, I hope, have provided some wisdom for these pages.

Contents

Introduction

THERE ARE MANY BOOKS on the market covering motivation, success, and many of the principles I have written about in this book. However, many of these books are written by people of multimillionaire or big-money status, and though many of their books are good and well written, I sometimes have a hard time relating to the authors and to what they are saying, because to me the author always seems to be on a level that is way up there, while I am on a level that is way down here. I consider myself just a regular person who through hard work and persistence has had success, and by writing this book I hope to reach regular people and relate to them on an equal level. I offer practical advice on how to be successful, and insight into what may be the lost arts of selling.

If you are a reader of any type of motivational books or materials, then much of what I am talking about will be familiar to you. Even though you may have heard some of this information before, it never hurts to hear it again. Hopefully, it will recharge you.

I don't claim that by reading this book you will become a millionaire, but I do feel that by reading this book and following the principles I describe, you can increase your income considerably. This book can help those who would like to go into business for themselves. It offers all the advice and knowledge at my disposal, including all the pros and cons of going out on your own. Whether you sell insurance, real estate, automobiles, barber supplies, or home repair kits, I believe you can profit from this book. Whether you are a stage or set decorator, a store manager, a beautician, a landscaper, an office worker, or a factory worker, I believe that there is something here that may interest you and help you, inspire you, and motivate you to better your life and better yourself at the job you have now. I think there is something in this book for everyone.

In this book, I describe many of my own true-life experiences and accomplishments, and I give you advice on how to accomplish your goals and desires. All of my accomplishments and experiences are absolutely true, and anything I suggest that you do, I have done myself. I pull no punches, I speak frankly, and I try to be honest.

I have a goal in writing this book, and that is for you the reader to benefit from even the littlest idea or bit of information you might glean. My goal is that when you finish reading, you will feel better about yourself, be glad that you read it, and better your lot in life because of it.

John J. Tassone

Chapter one

Success

W<small>HAT IS</small> S<small>UCCESS</small>? What does the word "success" mean to you? What do you think it means to be successful? If you look in the dictionary you will find that success is defined as "a favorable result or outcome," and "the gaining of wealth, position, and fame or other advantage." Most people associate success with money, and to some extent they are correct. They think that if someone has a lot of money, he is successful. However, I don't entirely agree with this type of thinking. I don't believe that just because someone has money he is necessarily successful.

Take, for example, someone who has never held a steady job and suddenly inherits a sizeable amount of money from a deceased relative. Take, for example, a relatively poor person who marries someone wealthy and now suddenly has access to a sizeable amount of money. Does this make either of these people successful? A man who has failed at everything he has ever tried, including several business ventures, stops at a grocery store and buys a lottery ticket for a dollar. He wins millions of dollars from that ticket. Does that mean he is successful, or does it mean he's just lucky?

Over the years I have pondered this question many times. I have known many people who for one reason or another had a lot of money. I have to be honest and say that some of them did not impress me the least bit, and I never thought of them as being successful. I have watched other people squander their money foolishly. A truly successful person is prudent with his money, because he would appreciate the work and effort it took to get it. On the way up the ladder, working toward my goals for success, I watched people pass me by on the way up their ladder, chasing after their goals for success, only to watch them fall back down as I eventually passed them by later.

I am not disputing the dictionary definition, but a long time ago, after giving the subject of the meaning of success much thought and consideration, I developed my own definition for what success is, or at least an expanded version of the dictionary's. In my version, I firmly believe that success is when you reach the point in life at which other people seek you out for your advice, your opinions, your help, and your guidance. It's when others come to you with their questions, and want to know how you would handle a certain situation or problem. When you reach that level, I believe you are either already successful or are on your way to becoming successful.

How do you get to that point in your life? It's not easy. If you want success, you have to work for it. First of all, you must strive to be the best that you can be in everything that you do, especially in your field of work. To be successful, you must be honest with people at all times. You must have integrity and always stay focused. You must be kind and polite to people, always be available to them, and always take the time to talk with them. When you see people years after you have conducted business with them, you don't want to be in a position where you have to run and hide. If you dealt with people using the values I have described, they will be happy to see you, and you will feel good upon seeing them. You may not always agree with the way someone is thinking, and even if you don't, before writing him or her off, try putting yourself in their shoes, and try to see their reasoning. Try to understand their thinking. Once you have grasped their point of view, you will have a better understanding of just how to reason with that person. It helps no one if you are a hot-tempered person who flies off the handle because if it's not your way, it's no way at all. You have to condition yourself to be calm and cool, and for some people that might take a little work. You may sometimes have to be a diplomat. When there is a problem to be solved or a decision to be made, you must have the ability to see the situation from all sides before you can make a correct decision. You may surprise yourself and find that sometimes your first impulse or your first answer wasn't the best one after all.

When I was a young man, I was quick tempered and quick to insist that I was right. As I grew older, I mellowed, became wiser, and realized that I didn't know it all. Over the years my wife, Catherine, has been a great influence on me in that area, because she has an uncanny way of listening to others, seeing things from their perspective, and giving them good solid advice. She has a very calming way about her, and much of it has rubbed off on me. When you are calm and sincere with people, you will find that you gain their respect. Once you gain a person's respect, they will more readily come your way for your help and advice.

Be true to yourself. You should know that there is always something for you to learn. Don't ever think you know it all. Whatever you are doing in life, whether you are working for someone or running your own business, learn all you can learn about the field of work you are in. Be the best that you can be in that field. Work steady and work hard, and if you have to, run that extra mile to get the job done. Again, I truly believe that when people come to you for your help, your opinions, and your advice, then you are on your way to becoming successful. Once you get to that point, the money side of success will usually follow.

In addition to having or gaining knowledge, becoming successful means that you must believe in yourself. You must think positive thoughts, have goals for your future, decide you are going to attain those goals, and have faith that you will. *Faith is a state of mind, and you become what you feed your mind.* If you dwell on negative thoughts, negative things will happen. If you dwell on positive thoughts, positive things will happen. Success comes to those who become success conscious. Failure comes to those who allow themselves to become failure conscious. Both poverty and riches are the byproduct of thoughts. Just like you feed your body the proper foods, you have to feed your mind the food of positive thoughts so that your mind will grow and become strong with positive impulses. *Successful people are people who form the habits of doing things that failures don't like to do.* You, and only you, control your own destiny.

Success comes easier if you live a clean life. Taking drugs and drinking alcohol to excess can damage your body and affect the way you think. Your body must stay healthy and so should your mind. You wouldn't knowingly feed your body poison, but when you do drugs or drink excessively, that's exactly what you are doing. An unhealthy body leads to an unhealthy mind. To be successful you must always be thinking clearly so you can grasp and utilize the steps to success as they unfold before you.

When you do gain the success and the money that you are seeking, people on the outside will say that you are lucky. They don't understand, and maybe never could understand, the hard work you put in and the sacrifices you have made to get to where you are. It has been said, "Luck is when preparation meets opportunity." When you are making money and everything is going right, and it seems like you can't do anything wrong, maybe there is some luck involved. Believe me, you wouldn't have luck if you didn't work hard, so therefore it's safe to say, "The harder you work, the luckier you get."

Levels of Success

Here are a couple of facts that may surprise you. Out of the entire working population in the United States, the number of people who earn $100,000 or more a year is less than 10 percent. Some people will argue that the figure is more like 5 percent, but I will be conservative and stay with less than 10 percent. A second fact is that 90 percent of the people making $100,000 a year or more are in sales of some kind.

These are startling numbers. Where do your numbers fall in comparison? What level of success are you at? Some people may look at these figures as depressing, because there are so many people who don't reach the $100,000-a-year mark. Other people may see these figures as encouraging: since there are so many people who don't reach the $100,000-a-year mark, that would mean there is plenty of opportunity for them to reach that level, with nobody standing in the way. We have all heard that old saying "The ladder of success is never crowed at the top."

Do you want to raise your level? Do you want to make more money? Even if you don't reach the $100,000 mark, wouldn't you like to be making more money than you are now? Maybe because of the knowledge you will gain by reading this book you will be encouraged, you will be inspired, and you will want to work at raising your level of income.

"Sales" Is Not a Bad Word

I mentioned that 90 percent of people making $100,000 or more each year are in sales of some kind. Some people hear the word "salesman" and they cringe. The fact is, this world of ours is built on sales. If nothing were ever sold, we would all be in big trouble, because none of us would have jobs and our entire economy would come to a halt. Every day, people buy groceries, clothes, gasoline, and thousands of other items. Somebody has to sell those items so that we may buy them. Whether you work in a sales-orientated business or a service-orientated business, if nothing was sold in this world, you would be out of work. Selling is the big engine that turns the world's economy, which depends upon people buying and selling goods. So the next time you hear someone talk down about a salesman, think twice, because that salesman may be helping you to keep your job.

Do You Live in a Jar?

Some time back an experiment was done in which a bunch of fleas were put in a jar and the lid put on. The fleas kept jumping up and down, trying to get out, and kept hitting the top of the jar. After a certain length of time, it was observed that the fleas were no longer jumping to the top of the jar and hitting it, and evidently quit trying to get out. The lid of the jar was then removed, and the study showed that even though there was nothing holding the fleas in, they quit jumping to the top of the jar and quit trying to jump out. The explanation for what happened is that the fleas were conditioned to their environment, and knew that they could only jump so high and not beyond. Due to the conditioning, they quit trying.

Over the years, experiments like this have been done many times using mice, monkeys, dogs, and a host of other living creatures, all producing pretty-much similar results. Humans are also living creatures, and they also can be conditioned. In fact, most humans are conditioned. They are what we call *average*. An average person is a run-of-the-mill, mediocre person, a so-so type. Average is what some people claim to be when their family and friends ask why they are not more successful. An average person is one who will never soar above the crowd to greater heights, and probably never stick his neck out to try. Why? Because of the way he has been conditioned. People are conditioned to believe that reaching for the golden ring is not for them, it's for somebody else. They are told they can't do it, and it's drummed into them enough so that they believe it. People are conditioned to accept their lives as they are, and to be content with being just mediocre. When people are conditioned in this manner, it's the same as living in a jar with a lid over their heads. They know that it's no use jumping up because they won't get out. They can only go so high, and then they quit. This, of course, doesn't have to be, but most people cannot see themselves moving out from the pack and becoming leaders, doers, and more successful than what they have been conditioned to be.

What's Coming Up?

In the following chapters, I will lay out what I feel are the ingredients of the formula necessary for success. I will explain in detail the subject of positive thinking, feeding on positive thoughts, and keeping negatives away from your front door. I will talk to you about believing in yourself and about setting goals — not just to say you set them, but deciding you are going to reach them. I will talk about some of the pitfalls you may encounter on your path to success, and give you clues on how to handle them. You will also find step-by-step methods for excellence at your workplace, the art of selling, tips on going into business, and the art of public speaking.

Please realize that everything I talk about is offered to you from my own beliefs, which have come about based on my own real-life experiences, failures, and successes. You may find that I will repeat more than once my ideas or suggestions regarding certain principles needed for success. I repeat these because they are important to you as you walk your path toward success, and I want to keep drilling at them so they leave a lasting impression in your mind.

Chapter two

Keeping Positive

Even a Broken Clock Is Right Twice a Day

To be successful in whatever field of work you are in, it will be necessary that you develop a positive attitude and that you keep that positive attitude about life, about yourself, and about everything around you. Being positive is not always easy. It may be something that you have to train for and work toward. You may have to practice being in a positive state of mind and maintaining that state of mind. You may have to learn to do things that can help keep you in that positive frame of mind. People want to deal with successful people, with people who have a positive attitude and are motivated, inspired, and enthusiastic. A positive attitude breeds success.

The reason I say that keeping a positive attitude may take work on your part is because we are surrounded by negatives. They are all around us, and every day we are bombarded by them. You have to learn how to avoid letting these negatives get to you. You have to learn to stay in front of them, and keep as much distance as you can from them. When you turn on the radio news or the TV news, all you hear are negative things. War, famine, disease, this person died or that child was shot, the economy is bad, gasoline prices are up, the jobless rate is rising, and dozens of other bits of bad news that certainly are not going to help you feel good or positive. If you read the newspapers it's no different. They are filled with depressing stories. When you are out on the streets or in a store, you may hear other people around you talking about their problems, their aches and pains, the lousy weather, some problem going on in the neighborhood, and anything else you can think of. It's no wonder you get depressed, and when you finally go to bed at night you want to give it all up.

The truth is, the TV networks could probably put a "good news only program" on the air, and people wouldn't watch it. We are all human, and we quickly grasp the negative thoughts before we grasp the positive thoughts. Also, there are many people who will gravitate toward the negatives. They like to hear about the bad things going on and all the gory things that happen. It justifies to them why their lives are so gloomy. The people who thrive on the negatives will never be positive or enthusiastic about anything, and therefore will not be the people who are successful. They are the ones who complain that life gave them a bad break.

You have to learn to look at positive things, think positive things, and find the positive things in the negative things that are thrown at you. Positive people usually turn out to be the successful people. It doesn't mean that you can never have a bad day, but you have to learn not to brood about problems and let them hold you down. Life is going to throw punches at you. Life can be hard and hit you right in the gut. You have to learn to hit back. When problems occur, don't sit there saying "poor me"; get up and do something about it. You will also find that sometimes when you can't see the answer to a problem, no matter how hard you try, if you just step back and maybe wait a day, the answer will be right in front of you.

There is one other area where you are sure to encounter negatives, especially if you are starting out on a new career or business venture. This area involves your family, your relatives, and your friends. I will discuss this at length in the next chapter.

What You Can Do to Stay Positive

At this juncture I'm going to suggest several things you can do to keep yourself on that positive road to success. There are many things that you can do to stay positive, enthused, and focused.

◆ When situations arise, look for the good in them rather than focusing on the negatives. Is the glass of water half full or half empty? It's all in how you view it. Nothing is ever totally wrong. Even a broken clock is right twice a day. You can usually find some good in the bleakest of situations. The good is what you should dwell on. The person who dwells on the good and positive side of things is the person who usually becomes successful.

◆ I wouldn't advise that you stop watching the news on TV or stop listening to the radio or stop reading the newspaper. Nor would I suggest that you cut yourself off from the world. What I will say is that when you do listen to the news or read the newspaper, remember that this is the news media, and it's their job to sensationalize. When you listen to the news and hear all the bad things that are happening, remember that the stories you are hearing represent only a small fraction of what's going on in America. The great majority of the people in this country are honest and good, and this is the clientele you are going to pursue to build your success. So don't let the bad-news people get you down. Put your thoughts always to your future, and all the

13

good people you are going to meet, do business with, and become friends with.

- There are many fine books on the market today that can be of great help to keep you motivated. Read some of them. They will help you to develop a character within yourself that will be the positive thinking one.

- Look for and attend motivational meetings or seminars in your area on a periodic basis. These will help keep you charged and focused.

- Each morning look at yourself in the mirror and pump yourself up. Tell yourself that you are going to have a good day. Tell yourself that today you are going to go out and make money. Shout it at yourself, and get yourself excited. If you leave the house charged up, it's going to result in positive things happening.

- Find other people in the same field of work you are in, make friends with them, and form a support group. Get together once a week to discuss strategies, exchange ideas, and to pump each other up. Do not have meetings to dwell on the negatives or all the bad things that can happen. When you have a circle of friends like this, you can support each other, and when one of you is down, help pick him back up. In the end, because you are part of a group with mutual interests, you will go a lot further than if you just worked alone. Each group member can help keep the others positive and excited, and because of that, everyone will produce more and make more money.

- Stay focused on your goals. Believe in yourself, and have faith that you will accomplish your goals. Nothing can stop the man with the right attitude from achieving his goals, and likewise, nothing can help the man with the wrong attitude.

◆ Stay enthusiastic about what you are doing, and always be enthusiastic in front of others. Enthusiasm is contagious. When you are happy, when you are smiling with excitement about what you are doing, the people you come in contact with will become excited also. There is proof that if you walk into a crowded room smiling, everyone else in the room will smile with you. If you walk into a crowded room with a frown on your face, everyone else in the room will start looking sad also.

◆ Finally, talk to your God. Ask Him for help. Ask Him to guide you and keep you on the positive road to success. If you ask Him, He will listen.

The Hotdog Vendor

There is an old story about an elderly hotdog vendor who had a very successful business selling hotdogs. He never listened to the news on TV or radio, and he had no negative thoughts entering his mind. He sold hotdogs, he was good at it, and he made money. He would shout, "Buy a hotdog, mister," and people would buy. Then one day his son came home from college and brought his dad up-to-date on world affairs, the troubles in the country and in the world. He convinced his dad that the economy was in terrible shape and people were losing their homes. The old man listened, and his brain absorbed all the negative things his son was telling him. He became distraught and paranoid. He could no longer sell his hotdogs in the same enthusiastic manner in which he was used to selling them, because his mind was blinded by all the negatives it had taken in. He no longer shouted, "Buy a hotdog, mister." His business suffered because he was now a different person, but the only thing that changed was his own mind, his own thought process. Everything else in the world was just as it had been, but his business still went downhill until finally he shut it down. He could no longer see the positive things around him. He only looked at and concentrated on the bad. *My son was sure right,* he thought. *This world has a lot of troubles.*

This is a sad epitaph for anyone, but situations like this are real — they happen, and they happen every day.

Complacency

After you have been working at something for a period of time, and you have success at it, it is easy to find yourself falling into a complacent frame of mind. If you have people working for you, this complacency will travel down to those people, causing them to become complacent also, and production will slow down. You've been successful, so you say you're just going to stand back awhile. You quit thinking of new ideas, and you quit pushing yourself forward. You fall into a rut, and find that a rut is easier because it requires no thought. This is a pitfall that is more common than you think, but it's one you can't allow yourself to fall into, because this very thing has stopped a lot of potentially successful people in their tracks. When you have success with something, and you are on a steady forward path of growth, you develop a certain momentum. You must keep this momentum, and keep yourself moving forward at all times, leading yourself and the people working for you to greater productivity. When you slow down, even with the best of intentions, and lose your momentum, it is very hard to get it back again to the former level.

Even after you have cleared the hurdles and are on your way to success, there will be times when you need to recharge yourself and get back on the positive track. You can do this by practicing the "What you can do to stay positive" suggestions in this chapter. The key is that you must be smart enough to recognize when you could use recharging, and then recharge yourself.

> *Each morning you are given a new day. What you do with that day will be entirely up to you. You can waste it or use it for good. What you do with it is important because you are exchanging a day of your life for it. When tomorrow arrives, that new day will be gone, leaving in its place whatever you traded for it. You must always stay positive, and always look ahead at how you can make tomorrow a better day than today.*
>
> — Anonymous

Being a Leader

When you master the art of staying positive, and incorporate this into your everyday activities, you will prosper and become more successful. When you are a positive person, and know your stuff as it relates to your business or field of work, and people are seeking you out for your advice, you will not only become successful, you will also become a leader. Leaders have two important qualities: They are going somewhere, and they are able to persuade other people to go with them. Being a leader is what you want to strive for, because as a leader you will reap the lion's share of what life has to offer. A follower gets the leftovers and the crumbs. So remember: a leader, not a follower, is what you want to be.

When your business grows to where you have people working for you, they will be looking to you for leadership. They will come to you with their problems, and they will be seeking your help. It is extremely important that you stay focused and give them the type of guidance they deserve and expect. You have now become the person that you used to look up to when you were climbing your ladder to success. Lead your people right. Don't ever ask them to do something that you wouldn't or couldn't do yourself. After all, you are now the successful person that everybody else wants to be.

Overcoming Setbacks, Adversities, and Tragedies

In your life's path you are going to have setbacks, adversities, and possibly some tragedies. Unfortunately this is all part of life's struggle. If you are a leader, and I'm sure that you are, whether it be in your business field or at home, you will always have to stay strong, always keep your eye on what's ahead, and get your family and your people through the disparaging times.

I have had many setbacks, as I will describe, but the worst tragedy of all was when my daughter passed away unexpectedly at the age of thirty-three. There is nothing in the world that is harder than losing your child, and I wish it on no one. It would have been the normal thing to do, and no one would have faulted me, if I had just given up and said, "To hell with it all." But I couldn't allow myself to buckle. For several months I was in a daze; I felt like giving up, but I knew that many people were depending on me and were waiting for my cue. I had to be strong. I had to be the true leader so I could get my family through that terrible ordeal. I had to lead the way and help keep everyone's spirits up.

My business and my employees were also depending on me to lead. My problems could affect other people's lives, and I knew I couldn't let that happen. In the movie *The Godfather,* the singer Johnny Fontaine goes to the Godfather sobbing about a problem he is having. He cries to the Godfather, "What do I do? What do I do?" Don Corleone, played by Marlon Brando, slaps him across the face, grabs his shirt, shakes him, and shouts, "Be a man, be a man!" I remembered that line, and I knew I had to not only be a man, but had to be "The man," to help carry everyone else through that awful tragedy.

In your life, things will happen that you have no control over. You will have to be "The man" or "The woman," and stay strong and lead, because people are depending on you. You can feel bad and you can feel discouraged, but you have to be careful how you handle it and how you show it, because everyone will be watching you and following your lead. You have to look positive, stay positive, and keep your mind focused. If you don't, you will hurt everyone around you, and you will eventually destroy yourself. Remember, you don't drown by falling in the water — you only drown by staying there.

Chapter three

Believe in Yourself

So far we have talked about success, and how, to be successful, you need to have a positive attitude and keep the negatives away. The next ingredient in becoming successful is belief. You must believe in yourself, believe in what you are doing, and have faith that you will succeed. If you don't believe in yourself, no one else will believe in you either.

It's very hard to have belief if you are not knowledgeable about your products or your field of work. This knowledge is of the utmost importance. Learn as much as you can about your products and your field of work, and always keep on learning. When you are knowledgeable, you are confident. Confidence creates enthusiasm. Enthusiasm creates sales.

If you don't believe in yourself, it will be hard to have faith that you will succeed. If you don't believe in yourself, gaining and digesting the knowledge will be harder. You must believe that you are as good as anyone else and that you can be successful. There's an old saying: "All men put their pants on the same way — one leg at a time." So, if someone else can have success, then why can't you? You just have to apply yourself, have the desire to succeed, gain the necessary knowledge, believe that you can do it, and work your butt off until you reach your goal. Every man is what he is because of the thoughts that he permits to dominate his mind. It takes no more effort to aim high in life. The person who gets ahead is the one who does more than what is necessary — and keeps on doing it.

When I first started out selling life insurance, I was a young man, and I looked younger than I was. I saw this as a handicap. Since almost all the prospective clients I spoke to were older than I was, I thought they would look down at me, thinking: *What does this kid know about anything?* It didn't take long to realize I was wrong. I knew my product inside and out, and I learned a great deal about the life insurance industry. When talking to prospective customers, this knowledge showed through. There was no longer an age barrier. My fears were unjustified, and I made sales. I explained my product professionally, I was enthused, and I answered all their questions with confidence. I believed in myself and in what I was selling. I never feared the age factor again. I realized a very simple fact: I knew more about my product than the client did. Therefore I was the expert. This fact should hold true with you also. As long as you know your stuff, you will be the expert when it comes to your client.

I believed in my product. This is very important. You must believe in your product or the service you are providing, and you must believe that it will be good for your client. If you don't, your sales will reflect it. I have always lived by the motto that I couldn't sell anyone something that I wouldn't buy myself. If you adopt that same motto, you should never have a problem. On the other hand, I believe that when you purposely sell a product to someone that you know isn't the best for him, and you know he could do better, but you make the sale anyway just to get the money, it's the same as committing fraud. Always do your best for your clients, and always look out for their interests first. If you can adopt that attitude, your growth will come back tenfold, and you will go very far.

Negatives Can Be Relative

After graduating college, I became a high school mechanical drawing (drafting) teacher for the Chicago Public School System. I also taught at the Cook County House of Corrections, training inmates. I left teaching and became a draftsman for a large steel company located in downtown Chicago. At that time my knowledge of insurance was zero.

In September 1967 I was working full-time for the steel company. I was married, had two kids, bills, and a mortgage. To make ends meet, I worked two part-time jobs in addition to my full-time job. One job was three nights a week as a draftsman for another downtown firm, and the other was on weekends selling clothing in a men's store. I was wearing myself out. A friend of mine, Paul, came by to see me about a new opportunity. He told me there was a new life insurance company starting in Decatur, Illinois, with some new ideas, and they were looking for people to sell their products.

He explained that I would be required to go to a three-day weekend crash course, and pay $300 for the privilege. In 1967, that was a lot of money. Like anybody in his or her right mind I told him no. As I said, I knew absolutely nothing about insurance. It was something I didn't understand and didn't want to understand. I didn't want to be an insurance man.

Paul explained that the company had a money-back guarantee. If I sat through the three-day training and didn't think it was for me at the end, then my money would be returned. Paul drove a hard bargain, and I owed him a couple of favors. I reasoned that I could square myself with him by going to the school, and then at the end, say it wasn't for me, and ask for my money back. I saw it as a win-win situation.

I made arrangements to attend the school in Decatur, paid my money, and went. My wife was furious. She did not want me to go off on a stupid wild-goose chase and spend $300 to boot. Also, for some reason, she didn't want me to be an insurance man. However, I arrived there on a Friday morning and began my training. I was immediately impressed. There were three instructors who took turns with different segments of the course, and they were good.

The Decatur Company had a new idea: They sold a life insurance policy that gave you insurance coverage and also built up what was an unusually large amount of money for the times. After a certain number of years passed, depending on your age at purchase, because of the power of money, the policy would accrue to a point where the cash savings side actually became larger than the total amount of money you put into it, and would continue to grow from there on. The policy would pay for itself and still grow on the savings side. I had never seen anything like it and neither had anyone else. I knew this had great potential and was going to be a good seller. Looking back, I would say that this policy was a forerunner of what we now call universal life.

I was immediately hooked.

Because I was young and very naive about the business world, I looked at the three male instructors and, for some reason, thought they were millionaires. They never said they were, but they carried themselves with a very successful look about them, and that's what I believed. I said to myself, "If they could make it, why can't I? They look like just regular people to me, so why can't I do just as well, or even better?" This three-day school was a life-changing experience for me.

Friday night came and it was time to call home and break the news to my wife that I liked the school and had decided to pursue this as a career. I took a deep breath and made the call. My wife's sister, whom I will refer to as Jane, was married to Bill. The first thing my wife said to me was: "Jane called and said she and Bill don't want to buy any insurance, so don't call on them."

Can you imagine? Here I was, a young man trying to better myself in life and provide a better future for my family. Whenever you try something new, it's scary enough as it is, and you need all the encouragement you can get. Instead, the first words I heard were a big, fat negative. My sister-in-law and brother-in-law called to tell me not to bother them. It was devastating. Some people might have folded right then and there.

Because of an unbelievable coincidence, during the last hour of school that afternoon, the instructor told us to be prepared for negatives from our relatives and friends, and explained to us that they would be our toughest critics. He also told us what to say to them and how to handle the situation when it came up. At that moment I couldn't thank him enough for the knowledge he gave me. In answer to that deflating negative comment, I said to my wife: "Tell them not to worry. I never planned to ask Bill and Jane, because they wouldn't qualify for this program anyway."

The message got back to Bill and Jane, and after I started my new career, I purposely never approached them to buy. However, I always made sure they heard through the grapevine how good the program was and how successful I was becoming. There were several occasions when they tried to make conversation with me about it, but I would never give them the satisfaction of presenting the program to them.

It may sound like my ego got in the way of common sense, and that I was being really cold and stupid by not saying, "Okay, I'll tell you about the plan," and hopefully make a sale. Maybe my ego did get in the way, but when I came home from the three-day course, I received so much negative response and ridicule from my wife's entire family that I decided they weren't worth getting aggravated over. In fact when I arrived back home on Sunday night, I went to pick up my wife from her mother's house. Just coming out of a three day pump-up course, I was so excited about the future and what I'd just learned, and so confident that I was going to be successful, that I blurted out to my wife and mother-in-law that I was going to be a millionaire.

First they broke into laughter, then ridiculed me, and then went into a shouting tirade. They said I was a fool to think that I could better myself, and had just wasted $300. They told me insurance guys were a dime a dozen. Why would anyone want to buy from me, a nobody, when there were so many others out there? The hurt I felt was deep. I realized I would never have their support, and whatever I did in the business, I would have to do it alone. I made the decision at that time that this would be okay, because that's the way it was going to be and I had no control over it. Nonetheless, I believed in myself, had confidence in myself, and I felt strongly that I could be successful with or without their support. After all, I wasn't going to quit my day job. I was just going to give up the two part-time jobs and sell insurance part-time instead.

It wasn't long before I realized I really liked what I was doing, and started dreaming of the day when I could sell life insurance full-time. Meanwhile, I still had to put up with the negatives from home and family. The lesson to be learned here, if you can call it a lesson, is that when you decide to venture out and do something different to better yourself and give your family a better life, you might not get the encouragement from your family that you think you deserve.

I think this may be caused from something that's very basic in a lot of people. Let's take, for example, siblings, sisters-in-law, brothers-in-law, cousins, and friends. It isn't that they don't like you, and it isn't that they don't want you to succeed and be happy, it's that consciously or subconsciously, they don't want you to be more successful or happier than they are, and for sure they don't want you to make more money than they make. There might even be some jealousy coming into play. They might not even realize they feel this way, but in most cases they do. Later on, after you have gained success, they don't like you because you're "lucky," or you're the "rich" guy or gal. The truth is, these same people who point the finger would never work as hard as you, and would never make the sacrifices you have made to be successful. All they know how to do is criticize. I'm not implying that all families are like this, but we are human, and being what we are, it can happen. So, if it happens to you, don't let it knock you down and destroy your confidence or your dreams.

How Might This Affect You?

Now let's bring this closer to your home. If you're trying to start a new venture or move your life in a different direction, it is extremely important that you have your spouse backing you and cheering for you to succeed. If you're not married, then it could be your boyfriend, girlfriend, or your significant other. When you don't have the approval of your spouse or loved ones, success will be far more difficult to achieve. You will find yourself fighting two battles — the battle to build a successful business, and the battle at home. This is probably the hardest situation to be in, yet a great many people find themselves right up to their necks in it.

What do you do? There is no one answer I can give you, and no easy answer to that question. I will simply tell you how I handled the situation. I moved forward, and focused on what I wanted out of life and what I wanted to do. If all everybody wanted to do was criticize, ridicule, and scream and yell, that was his or her problem. I vowed that I would let no one talk me down or scare me into defeat. I believed in myself, and had faith that I could achieve my goals.

If you are the breadwinner in your house, whether you are a man or woman, the fact is you have to work every day. You probably will have to work for the rest of your life, so you'd better work at a profession you like and are happy with. If you don't, the days get very long, and you are just existing and going through the daily motions of your job. If you are not happy with what you do for a living, then you are dead inside and may not know it. Someone once said to me, "If you find a job or career that you like, you will never have to work a day in your life." That statement holds truth.

I repeat this, and I say it with meaning: If you are expected to work every day, most likely for the rest of your life, then you'd better work at something you like and are happy with. As long as your work is honest and not criminal, do not let anyone tell you what to do for a living. You are the one who has to work, so it had better be your choice.

Once I got the taste of selling the life insurance program and had some success doing it, I couldn't wait to get to the point where I could quit my job at the steel company and go full-time selling. When that alarm clock went off at six-thirty each morning, and I knew I had to go to work at the steel company, I would lie there and say to myself, *Oh, no, not another day.* In contrast, when I was finally doing insurance full-time, when the alarm went off, I would say, *Great — another day!*

28

It's a Wonderful Story

We have all seen the classic heartwarming movie *It's A Wonderful Life*, starring James Stewart. I'm sure we all agree it's a great movie. George Bailey, the character played by Stewart, suffers a terrible financial crisis, which could seriously hurt his family and all the people who believe in him. He decides the world would be better off if he'd never been born, and makes a wish to that effect. An angel comes down and grants his wish. George gets to see how the world would be if he was never in it. When the angel reverses the wish and puts George back into existence, he has a whole new appreciation for what's really important and what isn't, and a new set of values. He sees just how important a role he played in so many people's lives, and how their lives would not have been the same without him.

Look at yourself, and review your own life. Realize how many people you touch each day in one way or another, and the ripple effect it has on everything they touch because you were there to touch them. Your life is an epic story in itself, whether you want to believe it or not. You won't ever know how many people will be touched because of the things you do each day. Don't ever think your life is useless or worthless. Believe in yourself, and know that your journey through life can affect hundreds or thousands of people in one way or another. You are important, so as you travel life's path, do it with your head held high, because everything you do affects others.

Know your path in life, and know where you are going. Don't stop to look around because you think the grass might be greener somewhere else. It probably isn't. You are important — don't ever forget it, and don't ever give up. Instead of worrying about whether the grass is greener elsewhere, devote all your efforts to improving your life and making it the best that it can be for yourself and your family. Too many people depend upon you to do the right thing, so keep swinging even if you seem to miss more often than you hit.

There once was a man who had a rough go of it in life. He tried going into business and failed. He ran for the legislature and was defeated. He tried business again and failed again. He ran for the legislature again, and this time was elected. His sweetheart died, and he had a nervous breakdown. He ran for public office eight more times and was defeated each time. Finally, he ran for the presidency of the United States, and this time he was elected. His name was Abraham Lincoln.

For decades, Babe Ruth held the record for the most home runs hit in a single baseball season. What many people don't know is that he also held the record for the most strikeouts in a season. Babe knew that if he never swung the bat, he wouldn't hit, so he kept swinging. He never gave up, and neither should you. Believe in yourself and have faith in yourself. Keep yourself enthused. Keep a positive attitude, and don't let the negatives get to you. Success isn't far away, and the world is depending on you.

Chapter four

Must Have Goals

The next ingredient in the formula for success is the setting of goals. You can be positive and enthused and believe in yourself, but if you don't have a goal, you will not get very far in your chosen career. Think about what you want and where you want to be, and then set goals to help you get there. Some of your goals should be short range and some should be long range. When you have goals, good things happen.

Be practical and be specific. You don't want to say, "My goal is to have a million dollars." You might very well make a million dollars, but unless you win the lottery, you'll have to do it step by step. Regardless of what business or line of work you are in, set some short-range goals that you can achieve in a reasonable time.

When I first started out in my insurance career, my first goal was to write ten policies. My next goal was to bring that total to twenty-five. When I reached that goal, I reset my goal to fifty policies, and then to one hundred.

This would be a good pattern for you to follow, regardless of what you are selling. Set your first goal at getting ten clients, then twenty-five, then fifty, etc. Once you reach your first goal, and then your second, you will feel confident, and gain more confidence than you had before. You will find yourself more enthused and more aggressive. The more clients you get, the easier it becomes to get more. They will seem to breed each other. Make no mistake: the beginning is the hardest. You will have to work hard for the first twenty-five or fifty, but when you finally get to that one hundred mark, it seems to get very easy to gain more, and your success becomes assured.

For your long-range goals, start by setting goals of where you want to be in five years and ten years. In your mind's eye, see yourself already there, and make yourself feel that you are already there. Think about it every day. See it in your mind every day. Every day, pretend you are there already. There is a saying: "If you can see it in your mind, and believe you can achieve it, then you will indeed achieve."

Tips on Attaining Your Goals

This may sound repetitious, but it's so important you can't hear it enough. The most crucial tip I can give you for reaching your goals is to keep thinking about them. In your mind, start to eat, sleep, and breathe them. Become obsessed with the desire to reach them. Think about reaching your goals all the time. As you think, see the steps that you must take. If you keep practicing seeing and believing and thinking about your goals, good things will happen. Your thoughts and desires will settle into your subconscious mind, and your subconscious will start to work for you. It will start to guide you in the right direction. You will find yourself doing things that will lead you closer and closer to reaching those goals, things you would not have done if you weren't thinking about them all the time. I am not a doctor, psychiatrist, or scientist, so I can't explain the process.

I only know that it works. Your subconscious will guide you to things your conscious mind couldn't see. How do you keep your subconscious mind working for you? Keep feeding it thoughts from your conscious mind.

Make a list of your goals. Write them down on a piece of paper, and keep it where you will see it all the time. Make more than one copy so you can keep one at home, one at work, and one on your person. Go another step and tape a copy to your bathroom mirror. Now every morning, when you look in the mirror, you can read it and be reminded of your goals and get recharged. Look at yourself, pump yourself up, point at yourself in the mirror, and say, "Today I'm going to go out and make some money, and in the process, I will be a step closer to my goals." It might sound silly, but this type of exercise really works.

What If You Don't Meet Your Goals?

Not everyone who sets goals meets them, but this is not necessarily a bad thing. For sure there will be those who never get out of the starting gate. This is unfortunate, but the great majority of those people who don't meet their goals either never tried or gave up too early.

As you work toward your goals, the goals themselves can change because you obtain more knowledge along the way and may want to adjust your goals to something better or different.

Picture a diagonal line on a piece of paper, starting at the bottom left-hand corner, which we will call Point A, and ending at the top right-hand corner, which we will call Point Z. You are at Point A, and your goal is to get to Point Z. As you start your climb, you may wander off track and veer to the left or to the right. I will call that sidetracked. Sometimes, what you find when you've sidetracked like that may actually be better than the Point

Z you were originally aiming for. There is nothing wrong with going off track and aiming at a different goal, as long as you are indeed still aiming at a goal.

You may never reach your goal. Picture the diagonal line as representing the alphabet, with "A" at the bottom left, "Z" at the top right, and the letter "L" or Point L in the middle. You may wind up somewhere beyond or below "L," or anywhere else along the line, but higher than where you started, which was Point A. When you accomplish this, you will have succeeded in bettering your life. Remember, if you'd never aimed at Point Z to begin with, you would never have climbed at all, and would spend your life at Point A, so setting a goal definitely can and will better your lot.

I would never make a claim that if you read this book you will grow mega-rich, but the information in *Go For It!* can help you do better than you're doing now. If by reading this book, a person currently earning thirty, forty, or fifty thousand dollars a year elevates his or her income to sixty, eighty, or ninety thousand dollars, then this book will have done its job. This of course doesn't mean that you couldn't become a millionaire, but I like to keep things in perspective, and hope you are surprised.

Accidental Goals

Throughout history, thousands of people have had goals they never reached. They got sidetracked, but because they had goals, they changed their lives and, in some cases, the lives of all of us living today. Success stories abound; there are many examples of famous people who became famous by accident, and many examples of those not so famous.

◆ Christopher Columbus is best known for discovering America, and thank God he did, but that wasn't his goal. His goal was to find a faster route to the rich trade goods of the Indies by sailing westward around the world. He never accomplished that, but in the process of aiming for his goal, he discovered America. That was his accidental goal. On our diagonal line, Columbus wound up at Point L. If Columbus hadn't had a goal, and if he'd never tried, we might all be living in Europe right now.

◆ Alexander Graham Bell set out to invent a hearing aid to help his deaf mother. In the process, he accidentally invented the telephone. In the case of Mr. Bell, his goal was a hearing aid, and his accidental goal was the telephone. Eventually, however, he did reach his original goal and developed the hearing aid, but good thing there was an accident. How would we text today if there wasn't?

◆ In the mid-nineties, my friend, Clim, opened up a beauty supply store for a friend of his to run and operate. I insured the store for him. The business didn't do well, and failed after two years. Clim called to tell me he was shutting down and that I should cancel the insurance. Of course I told him that I was sorry to hear the business didn't make it, and I asked him what he was going to do with all the merchandise he had left. He explained he was filling boxes with all the items he thought barbers might be able to use, like combs, powders, scissors, etc., and was going to drive down the street, stop at every barbershop he saw, and try to unload the stuff.

An incredible thing happened when he walked into the first shop: The barber said, "Where have you been all these years?"

You see, the only suppliers of barber products at that time were located in downtown Chicago. They had no competition, so all the barbers had to go to them. This meant that almost every week, barbers on their off day had to travel downtown to buy their supplies. If you know anything about downtown Chicago, you know that this takes anywhere from half a day to all day. Clim was like a breath of fresh air to these barbers. They asked him if he had this or that, or if he could get this or that. When he called me the next day to tell me what happened, I was elated for him, and I knew he'd struck gold.

Clim saw the potential immediately. Before long he got himself a truck, loaded it with barber supplies, and drove from barber to barber selling his goods. He developed a barber supply store on wheels. Soon he had two trucks, employees, and an established route consisting of over 200 barbershops. His original goal was to unload his merchandise, even at a loss if need be. That goal accidentally turned into a full-fledged successful business. Clim has since sold his barber supply business and has very success-fully moved on to the manufacturing side of the barber supply business, concentrating on newer and better razors, blades, and clippers. All this happened because he wanted to unload some merchandise.

- About twelve years ago, another client of mine, Rick, called to tell me he was going to be late making his insurance payment because he'd lost his job at the hardware store. He said he was looking for work but was having a hard time finding a job because the economy at that time was down. He asked me if I had any suggestions for him to make some money until he found a job.

I pointed out that since he worked in a hardware store, he must have gained some knowledge that he could put to use. I asked him if he knew how to seal coat a driveway, paint a bedroom or garage, put up outside Christmas decorations on homes, mow a lawn, or one of many other everyday things that the average homeowner might use him for. His answer was yes to all of them.

I suggested he make up a flyer listing all the things he was capable of doing, and blanket the neighborhood with them. I said that every home needs something to be done or fixed, and if he presented himself, people might just call on him for his services. The response to his flyers was astounding. After a while, he scaled down to just painting, and today runs a successful painting and decorating business with employees. His goal was to find some fill-in work until he could find a job. That goal accidentally turned into a successful business.

Since then, I have made that same suggestion to several others who were out of work, and today, after finding their own niches, run successful businesses.

◆ Some time back, one of my customers was in my office paying his insurance premium, and in conversation told me an incredible success story. He had a son who didn't like school, didn't like homework, and didn't like to study. All the kid wanted to do was play video games. His father said that every night he would holler at his son, but to no avail. The boy would ditch school to sit home and play video games while his parents were at work. He was addicted to them. His father was pulling his hair out, concerned as to what his son would do in life.

Somehow the boy did manage to graduate high school, and, to his father's great surprise, made a connection with a video game manufacturer who hired him to play video games. His job was to play, test, and analyze the new games being developed, for market appeal. They started him at $80,000 a year.

I can't say what his goal was, if he had one, or even understood the meaning of a goal, let alone what his accidental goal was, but this story was so good I just had to tell it.

- I have many success stories, but this is by far one of my favorites. I originally saw it on the Biography Channel, and it impressed me so much, and it's such a feel-good story, that I thought I would include it here. Back in 1969 an aspiring author was living in New York and striving to be successful. He was married and had several children. He was of Italian descent and he believed that his name and fame would be secured if he wrote a definitive book consisting of several volumes on the history of Italy from the time the world began to the current day. He thought this would put him in the *Who's Who of Authors and Writers*.

To make ends meet, he wrote short stories and mediocre books for a local publisher. He had to guarantee them a certain amount of publishable work in certain time frames to keep his contract. As time went by he became so obsessed with writing his history of Italy, and spent so much time doing it, that he fell way behind on his obligation to the publishing company. Before long, they were on his back, threatening to end the arrangement. He asked for time, and promised he would get them something. He couldn't afford to lose the income because he still had bills to pay and a family to support, and was barely scraping by as it was.

Very grudgingly he set aside his history work, sat down at his typewriter, and started composing a story so he could get the publisher off his back. He worked diligently day after day, and after about six weeks finally finished a book. He was so anxious to get back to his history volumes that he didn't even want to take the time to deliver his work to the publisher. His brother-in-law happened to stop by, so he gave him the book and asked him to deliver it for him. The brother-in-law delivered the book, and a couple of days later the author learned that the publisher had "really" liked it.

The name of the book was *The Godfather*, and the author was Mario Puzo. I don't have to elaborate on what his accidental goal was, because the rest is history.

◆ Using myself as an example, my original goal was to go to Decatur, Illinois, to an insurance school in order to get Paul off my back. I had every intention of asking for my money back, but here I am, forty-four years later, successful in a business I thought I wanted no part of, and writing a book to tell you about it.

Summary

It's always helpful and enjoyable to hear stories of success. I hope these few examples will serve to excite and encourage you. There are hundreds and thousands more. You yourself probably know of several, and may even know the people involved. Remember, none of the people I have talked about, and none of the people in the success stories you know, would have ever achieved their success if they weren't out there swinging and working every day, and if they hadn't had some type of goal. A goal is the one thread they all have in common.

Do not procrastinate. Many people go through life as failures because they are waiting for the "time to be right" to start doing something. The time will never be "just right," so start now to achieve your goals and work with whatever tools and whatever knowledge you have at your disposal.

I have told you to set goals, believe in them, believe in yourself, work hard, and you can achieve a greater place than where you are now. I believe this, and I hope you do also. Goals work. Remember: when you have goals and work hard, good things will happen.

Chapter five

Decide You Are Going to Do It

It has been said that there are three types of people in the world: those who make things happen, those who watch things happen, and those who wonder what happened.

This subject, "Decide You Are Going to Do It," was originally to be part of the chapter on goals. However, as I progressed in my writing, I decided that it warranted a chapter of its own. I really want to stress its importance, so I devote this chapter to it. You have to set your goals, and then DECIDE you are going to reach them. That is the whole key.

Everything we have talked about so far is very important, and each topic we have discussed is an important ingredient in the formula for reaching success. You can be positive and enthused, you can be negative-free, you can believe in yourself, and you can have goals. All of those are important, but if you don't decide that you are going to reach those goals, then you may become stagnant.

What I'm trying to say is, you not only have to *tell* yourself you are going to succeed, you have to *convince* yourself you are going to succeed. You have to know it throughout your entire body. You have to convince your mind, which in turn will convince your subconscious that you are going to do it. When individual people, or groups of people, make the decision to succeed, there is no looking back, and mountains can be moved. The power of decision is one of the strongest powers on earth.

You can't sit back and say, "I'd really like to do that" or "I hope I can do it" or "That's my goal and I want to achieve it." You have to say to yourself, "I'm going to do it," with confidence and belief in yourself that you will indeed do it, and you must know that no other option will be acceptable.

A Super Example

I'm not a great sports fan, but I do like football. Born and raised in Chicago, I am, of course, a Chicago Bears fan. I remember vividly the 1985 Chicago Bears as they played through the season, winning all the regular games but one, then on through the playoffs and then the Super Bowl, which they won easily.

The Bears team that year was explosive. They decided from the season opener that they were going to go all the way to the Super Bowl. It wasn't "We hope we can win" or "Maybe we can win"; it was "Yes, we can win, and we are going to get there." It was never "IF we get to the Super Bowl"; it was "WHEN we get to the Super Bowl."

As you watched the Bears play, you could see in the faces and in the eyes of the players, a determination and sureness about themselves, and you could see that, mentally, they were already at the Super Bowl. They just had to go through the formality of playing the regular-season games and the playoff games first. I am sure that there was never a doubt in any of the players' minds that they would be Super Bowl champs. You can probably still obtain a video or DVD of the 1985 Bears, in which you'll be able to see what I'm talking about.

When people talk about sports, whether it's football, baseball, basketball, or other, they will inevitably bring up the extravagant paychecks many athletes receive. You may also hear it said that the money is going to be paid whether they win or lose, so why should they care about giving it their all. This may certainly be true with some athletes, and to be sure, we have all seen players who didn't seem to even know what the ball looked like, but going back to the 1985 Chicago Bears, that wasn't the case. All the players were receiving big money at the time, but as a team they went above and beyond what was expected of them. Yes, the money was there, win or lose, but it was no longer a matter of money. They wanted to win, they decided to win, and money or no money, nothing was going to stop them.

You don't have the luxury of getting paid whether you deliver or not. You have to work, so why not work with a burning desire to be the best you can be, and decide to reach the goals you have set for yourself?

An American Example

One of my passions is American history. For me, it's a fascinating study. Throughout our history, from the time the Pilgrims landed, right on up to today, our people and our country have overcome adversity and obstacles, and have many times faced defeat right in the eye and stared it down victoriously. The American spirit is one in which defeat is not an option. We as a people may fight and argue among ourselves over various issues, but when there is a national crisis, we come together with a will and desire and a purpose to win like no other country in the world.

The Second World War was one of the greatest tests this country ever faced. After World War I, the American people were tired of war. We as a country became complacent. The size of our military shrunk year after year, and Congress wasn't doing anything to reverse the trend. People didn't want to be involved in Europe's problems.

In 1937, our American military ranked nineteenth in the world, behind Poland. There is an old *Life* magazine photo from the year 1938. It was spread over two pages, and was an aerial view of what the magazine said was one half of our entire mechanized military. I counted the vehicles, which consisted of trucks, tanks, and jeeps. I counted 146 in total, plus, about a dozen motorcycles. If that is indeed how unprepared we were back in 1938, then that is pretty scary.

When the Japanese attacked Pearl Harbor on December 7, 1941, it galvanized America. Overnight, the American people came together to answer the call. Every American wanted to know what he or she could do to help. The next day, the Philippines fell, and the next few months brought nothing but bad news to our homes. We and our allies suffered setbacks and defeats. We were fighting for our survival, but the resolve at home never faltered. From our political leaders to the everyday citizen, no one ever said, "I hope we can win this war" or "If we win the war." Instead, people said, "WHEN we win the war." Our people and our country set a goal to win the war, believed they would win it, and made a DECISION to win it. Once that decision was made, there was no stopping us.

Before the war, it took seven months to build a single ship. By 1944, America was building fifty ships a day, and in addition, eight aircraft carriers each week. We were producing one tank every fifteen minutes and one airplane every five minutes.

In one airplane plant alone, raw materials would be delivered by rail to one end of the plant to be melted down and processed, while at the other end of the plant, a new airplane was rolling out every thirty minutes. When the Japanese lost a plane, they couldn't replace it. When we lost a plane, we had ten more to take its place.

In addition, we produced thousands of jeeps, thousands of trucks, millions of guns and rifles, billions of bullets, and a multitude of other items needed for the war. We not only supplied our own military with the equipment they needed to win the war, we supplied our allies also.

The whole point I am making is, when America as a nation DECIDED it was going to win the war, the people of America rolled up their sleeves, went to work, and won. Losing the war was never an option. We out fought the enemies and out-produced them at the same time.

A Business Example

In my business, I have attended a lot of meetings held by insurance companies. At each and every one of them, the company representative stands before the group of insurance agents, trying to encourage them to sell more of this or more of that. The representative will try to psych them up by giving them goals. I sit there and watch the various insurance agents as they all agree to aim for the goals. They will make statements such as, "That's good, I want to do that" or "Yeah, I'm going to give that a shot" or "That sounds good."

When the meeting is over, all the agents agree they are going to meet the goals. The problem is they never really decide that they will do it. By the time they arrive back at their own offices, other pressing matters are waiting for them, they get busy, and soon forget all about the new goals they agreed to. At the next meeting, a few months later, the company representative is repeating himself all over again.

I don't fault the insurance agents; they are just human. Whether the company is selling insurance or automobiles or time-shares or whatever other product you can think of, the same scenario exists and repeats itself. No company is immune.

Pep Talk for the Mind

Not everyone has the discipline to decide he is going to succeed, or the stamina to stay with it until he does. It's what separates the really successful people from the people of mediocre success and the wannabes.

When you look in the mirror each morning and tell yourself you are going to go out and make some money today, or you tell yourself you are going to reach your goals, say it with conviction. Tell yourself you are going to do it. Think about it each morning, during each day, and when you go to bed at night. Drill it into your subconscious, so that your subconscious mind will start doing the work for you and guide you to your goal.

Each night when you go to bed, review your day's activities. Evaluate yourself. Did you do all that you could? Are you any closer to reaching your goals? Are you happy with the day's results? If you were your boss, would you be happy with the job you did today? If not, take steps for self-improvement.

You don't just set goals and then sit back and wait for them to happen or expect them to happen without any effort. You have to exert yourself, you have to work, and you have to make things happen.

If you go on a diet to lose weight, you don't just go on it for a day or two. If you go on an exercise program to firm up and tune up your body, you don't stop after just a few days. Whether it's a diet, an exercise program, or any other challenge, you have to stay with it for as long as it takes to get the job done. You check your weight or your muscle tone each day to monitor your results. Even though it might be a slow process, you still hope to see some type of positive result each time you check.

You have heard the expression "A mind is a terrible thing to waste." You have to exercise your mind each day. You must keep feeding your mind the image of yourself already at the place where you want to be, and already in possession of the money you desire, as if you were already there. You have to keep telling your mind each day, all day, that you want to reach your goals. That mind exercise will tone up your subconscious to keep working for you. By doing this every day, you will condition your subconscious mind to carry on and bring you to where you want to be.

Just like the saying "A quitter never wins and a winner never quits," you must never quit thinking and believing that you will achieve your goals. The people who stay the course make things happen. The others watch and wonder what happened. YOU be the one in your family to make things happen.

Chapter six

Give That Man a Pat on the Back

As you begin reading this chapter, your first impression might be that I am bringing negatives into this book. That is not my intention. I am, however, going to discuss negative situations, which are real in business, corporations, and the general workplace. I hope you will never experience any of what I'm going to discuss, but situations like this do exist. I learned firsthand just how people can turn against you in the workplace, and how hurtful it can be. It's my hope in this chapter to make you aware, to open your eyes to real situations that could come your way, and how to handle them.

I could never understand why some people in management feel intimidated if someone under them is shinning bright and doing a good job. Instead of encouraging them, and maybe even taking credit for being a good leader, they will look for ways to muffle, squeeze out, or even fire that person. This kind of thinking is stupid and destructive. It does no one any good, but only serves to destroy enthusiasm and momentum, and ultimately cost everyone money.

Management may not be the only culprit in these situations. The same negatives and jealousies may also come from coworkers who may be fearful that you might excel, pass them by, and be more successful than they are. They may talk down about you to others, and, consciously or unconsciously, even try to sabotage your performance. They are human, and sometimes this is how humans behave.

My Experiences with the Decatur Company

In September 1967, I entered the insurance field with the Decatur Company on a part-time basis. I was twenty-four years of age, and I was fired up. I worked hard and sold policies. After one year, I was making more money part-time than I was making full-time at the steel company. I had a choice to make, and I made it. I quit the steel company. Before I left, my supervisor called me into his office and berated me for being so foolish as to leave such a good job. He told me I was making a big mistake and that I would never make it in insurance, because insurance men were a dime a dozen. He assured me that after one year I would be back on my hands and knees, begging for my job back. Just to show you that you should never put all your faith in large corporations, a year later, in a consolidation move, the steel company closed its downtown Chicago office, and several hundred people lost their jobs. So much for me making a big mistake.

When I went full-time into insurance with the Decatur Company, I was promoted to district manager, with about twenty agents under me. I worked hard, I became a leader to my agents, I encouraged and helped them, and my district led all other districts in production and sales. I was becoming a true leader.

The Decatur Company was doing well. The Chicago area, with all its population, was beginning to grow and blossom. The Chicago area grew to the point where there were over twenty districts, each with a district manager, and over 400 agents. The area needed a leader, and the company decided to name a regional vice president for the northern third of Illinois. Everyone was looking at me.

I should have known then that my troubles were starting. There were clues, but I wasn't watching. The management in Decatur was typical of management in many large companies. They get so caught up with themselves they forget that it's the soldiers in the field who are doing the real work, and they begin to think they are invincible. Management consisted of a president, an executive vice president, and a senior vice president. After them, there came at least five junior vice presidents with different titles.

There is a saying that pertains to companies involved in sales: "If the guy can't sell, put him in management." I was dealing with people who couldn't sell, and couldn't even begin to do what I had already done. However, management felt they had to control me and keep me under their thumb. To them, I guess I was a loose cannon. As a control test, they sent my old friend, Paul, who was one of the five junior VPs, to tell me that the senior vice president was coming to town in the morning to appoint a regional vice president. I was told the job was mine if I did one simple thing — I had to shave my mustache.

I was floored. I felt like someone had knocked the legs out from under me, but I was young, still learning about business, and very naive about people. I didn't understand things like corporate insecurities and jealousies. I thought we were all supposed to work together, cheer each other on, and build an empire.

I wanted the job so badly I could taste it. That night I grudgingly shaved my moustache. The next morning I got the job. By the time I got home I was mad at myself. I felt like I'd sold out my principles. I felt violated. What on earth did a mustache have to do with making sales and leading a sales force? I immediately developed a strong distaste for the management — I didn't like them anymore.

I decided that now that I had the job, it would be hard for them to take it away from me. Too many agents looked up to me and followed me as I led them to sales and success. How could management explain that they let me go? I decided to let the mustache grow back. A month later, when I was in Decatur at a meeting with just the three big guys and me, they realized I'd grown it back. I decided not to act a fool and blame them; instead, I smiled and said that Paul told me I had to shave my mustache to get the job, and that the order had come from the home office.

I assured them that I realized it was probably just Paul's idea of what he thought they might want, and I knew that none of them would be small-minded enough to suggest such a thing. I could see the three big guys squirming in their chairs, but none of the three had the guts to say he'd given the order. They did the only thing they could: they agreed with me and blamed it on Paul.

So now the guy with the mustache set out to build the biggest and best region the Decatur Company had ever known. Over the next two years we hired more and more agents, both men and women. I always believed that women could sell insurance just as well as or better than men. We built a mini-empire in the Chicago area. For over two years straight, my region produced two-thirds of the company's entire business. What we were selling was a $10,000 face-amount policy with several special features, and each and every week my region wrote over one hundred policies. We had a system for delivery of the applications. As the agents wrote policies, they would turn them over to their district managers. Every weekend the managers would deliver the applications to me. Every Monday morning, I drove to Decatur and delivered a brown grocery bag filled with applications to the company. Each week, there was over $1 million worth of insurance, with checks amounting to between thirty and forty thousand dollars. We were like a snowball rolling downhill — the faster it rolls, the bigger it gets, and the bigger it gets, the faster it rolls. I felt like I was king of Chicago.

You would think that from then on we would all live happily ever after, but it didn't work that way. I had new troubles.

Agents sold policies in all the traditional ways that policies have been sold for years, like the in-home appointment. We took it a step further. The company held dinner meetings. An agent could bring his or her prospective client to a scheduled dinner meeting to hear about an opportunity. There was no obligation, and all the clients were assured that no one would try to sell them anything. Usually, there were thirty to forty people at a meeting, and none of the prospective clients really believed that no one was going to try to sell them something.

The agent paid for the dinners for his or her clients, and after dinner a qualified speaker gave the presentation. That speaker was usually me. I may sound vain here, but I was good. I would explain the program with enthusiasm, and by the time I was finished, every prospective client wanted one. Then I came in for the close. I would thank them all for coming, and ask that they drive carefully on the way home.

People couldn't believe it. No one tried to sell them. In fact it was our policy never to make sales at a meeting. The clients would want to know how they could get one of those policies, and I would tell them to talk to the person who had invited them. Usually, the next day, the agent would go to their homes and write the policies.

As my territory grew, we did better and better. I was now well known throughout the company, and was liked by many people. The "Home Office Three" began to squirm again because they had to answer to the board of directors and the chairman of the board. They got nervous when anyone looked too good, especially if they couldn't control him — and they couldn't control me. I was my own man, but even so, I always thought company first.

I was speaking at dinner meetings at least four nights per week. That, combined with holding managers' meetings, selling at least one policy per week myself, and helping others to sell, was a full workload. The home office appointed another man from my region to share some of the speaking load. We will call him Mike. He was much older than I was, and had been in the insurance business for many years. To Mike, I was just a young upstart. He didn't like me, and always felt that he should have been the man in charge of the region. Because Mike didn't like me, the home office liked him. They figured he could keep me in check and diminish some of the so-called power they thought I had. In fact, they had him spying on me and reporting all the good gossip back to them. The problem was, Mike was a horrible speaker. His audiences went to sleep. When an agent was paying for dinner for his client and the client's wife, he expected to make a sale. The presentation was key. So when the schedule of meetings was posted each month, showing who was scheduled to speak, the agents booked my meetings and not Mike's. This just added fuel to the fire. As far as good gossip was concerned, I unknowingly supplied him with plenty. After I became a regional vice president, and was running here and there, my wife and I divorced. It was 1972. Back in those days, the man usually took the beating in a divorce, but as I said earlier, no one was going to tell me how to work for my living. In the process, I became broke again.

Compared to all the other management people in the company, I was young. Now all these older married guys were looking at me, a young single guy, making money, driving a new convertible, and back on the dating scene. I was what they all wished they could be, and they hated me for it.

Mike took my situation and ran with it. He blew things out of proportion. He had me doing things I never dreamed of, including drunken episodes. Anybody who knew me knew I didn't drink, but this was music to the home office's ears.

As I said earlier, when companies get big, they sometimes forget how they got there. They start to believe they can do anything and still be as strong as ever. This company was dead wrong.

I was so caught up with building my territory and writing business, I was oblivious to what was going on. I didn't want anybody's job; I just wanted to do mine. One Monday, as I delivered my grocery bag of applications to the home office, I was called into a meeting room with the big three. Also present were one of the junior vice presidents and Mike. I was puzzled as to why he would be there, but it didn't bother me. I was in a good mood, I had just delivered another bag of life applications, and I thought they were going to tell me what a good job I was doing. Boy, was I wrong.

There was a long conference table in the room. I was told to sit at one end, and everyone else sat at the other end. From out of nowhere they started ripping me apart. It was mostly the president and senior vice president doing the ripping. The executive vice president seemed like his heart wasn't in it, but he let everyone else talk.

I was told that the company was not happy with my performance, and my job was on the line. They said there were reports of me going on drunken binges and carousing with women, and supposedly many of my agents had been complaining. For me, this was coming out of nowhere. I didn't know what hit me. I stammered and stuttered to no avail. I was in shock. I didn't even know how to begin defending myself against the charges they were making. I demanded to know the names of agents who were complaining, but they refused to say. My mustache came into play again. They told me that an "Italian from Chicago with a mustache" wasn't necessarily the image they were looking for in a vice president. Now, coupled with all these new accusations, I was told I really had to straighten out or be replaced. I felt sick and I felt insulted.

I was in so much shock that I began to cry. Tears were rolling down my face. Here I was, a grown man, crying in front of my superiors. I felt humiliated, and a silent anger was building up inside of me. I was directly or indirectly responsible for two-thirds of the company's business, and instead of being praised I was being beaten down. The junior vice president came over to me, sat down beside me, and tried to explain how they just wanted to get me back on the right track, since I had supposedly strayed off of it. The junior VP was a nice guy, but when I looked at him, I thought, *I bring in over a hundred policies a week, and this guy couldn't sell machine guns to General Custer at the Little Big Horn, yet here he is, ironic as it sounds, telling me how to do my job.*

Suddenly, it all hit me, and I saw the light. In a split second I figured out what was happening. I realized that Mike had set me up, and this was a kangaroo court. In that same split second, a hundred thoughts raced through my mind, and I knew exactly what I was going to do.

I wiped the tears from my face and stood up. I leaned over the table, looked them in the eyes, and confirmed that, yes, I was a single man and had been dating some girls, but that was limited to Saturday nights, because the rest of the time I was too busy seeing to it that my territory had its hundred life apps for the week. I held up the grocery bag and showed it to them as a reminder. I told them that the rumors about me being drunk were lies, because I didn't drink. If I took a woman to a lounge, I drank Seven-Up.

I let them know they didn't have to tell me which agents had complained, because I'd figured it out. There was only one, and he was sitting in the room. I pointed at Mike. I told them that Mike had had it in for me because the agents followed me and not him. They didn't want to use his dinner meetings because when they did, they wouldn't sell, and when an agent is paying for dinner he needs to make the sale. When they attended my meetings, they made sales. How else did they think we got the production every week?

Now I felt strong, and was getting stronger. I had already made up my mind as to what I was going to do, and I knew exactly how to do it. I assured everyone that I got the message, loud and clear, and would go back home and straighten out my act. I told them, "I see the light," and I thanked the junior vice president for putting me back on the right track.

The room seemed pleased. They thought that now they would have me where they wanted me, jumping through hoops when they said, "Jump." They were all beaming, except for the executive vice president. I could see on his face and in his eyes that he knew they had just screwed up big-time. He was starting to look sick. He had a bad feeling that in five stupid minutes they had just lost Chicago. As I was leaving, he followed me out of the room and tried to smooth things over. He praised my good work and told me he was looking forward to seeing more. He said not to get too upset about the meeting because they were just trying to help me. He tried to put a positive spin on a very ugly situation. I assured him I was okay, and left. During the three-hour ride back to Chicago, I put together all the steps of my plan to start a new life insurance company. By this time in my career, I knew lawyers, actuaries, and accountants. I knew what was involved in starting and building a life insurance company, and I was ready to do it.

When I returned home, my heart was no longer able to work for the Decatur Company. I couldn't be a hypocrite to my managers, agents, or the people. I had to tell them what happened. I never drove back to Decatur again. I resigned shortly thereafter. Dissatisfaction and doubt ran through the territory. The bubble was broken, and the company's momentum in Chicago slowly came to a halt. There were a few who thought they could capitalize on my misfortune, but they could never get any substantial production going. Once you lose momentum, it's almost impossible to get it back. The company lost two-thirds of its new business over stupid gossip and small-mindedness. A few years later, the company sold.

Triumph, Another Setback, and Triumph Again

By the time I got to Chicago, I had already made my plans. I spent the next few weeks visiting businessmen whom I knew, getting them to invest, and with them put together $375,000 to use as a base for the company. After the base was completed, we went public with a stock sale, using the dinner-meeting concept, and raised another $1,750,000. I was the speaker at all of these meetings. At the beginning of 1974, we sold our first life policy. I will refer to this company as the Oak Lawn Company.

As it turns out, I still wasn't as smart as I thought I was. When setting up the corporation, the lawyer suggested that I have a contract with the company, so that in the event the board of directors wanted me out, they would have to pay for it. I told him absolutely not. I said I knew these people, we were all friends, and I wouldn't insult them by demanding a contract. You see, the way I was raised, my word and handshake was a contract, and I believed that all the principal investors thought the same. I always believed that a person's word is the most important thing that person has, and if a person's word is no good, then there isn't much else good about that person either.

The company hit the ground running. I was CEO, and ran the day-to-day operations. I sold policies, trained people in how to sell, spoke at all the dinner meetings, and ran our monthly motivational meetings. In short, I worked day and night. The hard work paid off. In the first year we were a $20 million company. After two years we doubled. We were hot. We were using a company of independent nurses to give life insurance physicals. These were very bright ladies, and somehow they arranged for a popular news announcer, Bob Petty, from Channel Seven Eyewitness News, to come out and do a story. He did a combined story highlighting the independent nurses, our life company, and me. I received a physical on TV. The popularity I was gaining began to make certain people in the company nervous. The company was riding high, and I was riding high again and just about to make some real money. That's when my troubles returned. It was like Decatur all over again.

In 1976, I was thirty-three years of age. I was still single, always had a new convertible, and was still dating when I could find the time. The big problem was that I was starting to make some real money. The board of directors, all of whom, by the way, I had handpicked, were considerably older than I was. They were all married men, and some not so happy. Jealousy crept in, and it spread like a cancer, especially where the money was involved. I made everything look too easy, and two very influential board members, who themselves had considerable money invested in the company, began to think they could run it better. They never felt I was doing a bad job, they just felt they could get someone else in there to do a better job, make the company grow faster, and at the same time control him. I had no financial clout at all, since I had only $15,000 invested — and that was borrowed. During the whole year I spent setting up this company, I'd had no income at all. I lived off credit cards and lines of credit. Now that I was about to pull ahead, the rug was pulled out from under me.

The two board members were very successful and respected businessmen, and because of this they eventually got to everyone else on the board. I knew the life insurance business better than any of them because I was the only one with an insurance background. I ran the company the way I saw fit, so it would grow, and I would not let anybody control me. I had about 200 agents and managers, many of them my old agents from the Decatur Company, and we had that very important thing called momentum again. But now, there was infighting on the board. Everyone didn't like this or didn't like that. After many board battles, which can drain the enthusiasm out of anybody, I was voted out. They bought out my stock for $22,000. I paid off the $15,000 that I had borrowed, and was left with $7,000. I was broke again.

The board brought in a silver-spooned talker to run the company. They thought they had the best man for the job, that he could take the company to greater heights; they thought they could control him, and they gave him a two-year contract. When it comes to the subject of contracts, he was indeed smarter than I was. He brought all of his buddies into the company, gave them all expense accounts, and milked the company for hundreds of thousands of dollars.

In the meantime, I didn't know what I was going to do. I lay around the house, brooding about my bad luck, and my money was running out. After a few weeks, I realized I had to do something because the only one who was going to help me was myself.

I went to church and found God and asked Him for help. I also picked up a book that had been given to me years ago. I had never read it, and figured it couldn't hurt to read it now. It was called *Think and Grow Rich*. It was written by Napoleon Hill in 1937, is still available, and is just as meaningful today as it was then. I would recommend it to everyone.

That book changed my life. I couldn't put it down. When I was done reading it, I was re-energized, and I knew I would never let anyone put me down again. I knew I was going to be successful, and I knew that the only one who could stop me was myself. I also knew that God was on my side.

I vowed to myself that I would never again build a company unless I owned or controlled it. I was tired of the corporate rat race, and just wanted a little "Ma and Pa" business. I looked upon my experiences with both the Decatur Company and the Oak Lawn Company as my college education in the world of business. I decided to open a full lines insurance agency, selling all types of insurance including auto, homeowners, business, life, and health. In the summer of 1976, I went into business. It wasn't easy starting from scratch. I starved for a long time, but I never doubted I would have success. Before I opened up, a friend of mine who was in the insurance business told me that it would take five years to get an agency to the point of making decent money. I didn't believe him. I thought that maybe he didn't know what he was doing; I was sure I would do it in a year. I will tell you, he was right. It takes five years to turn an agency if you are starting from scratch. Good thing I didn't believe him, because if I had, I might have been scared off. I worked hard and long. Over the years, my agency has grown, and, I have to say, has treated me very well.

Sweet Justice

By 1978 I had been operating my agency for two years, and was still struggling. That was also the two-year mark for the contract the Oak Lawn Company had given to the silver-spoon guy. The contract wasn't renewed. I was in my office one afternoon when Joe, one of the board members, stopped by. I was very much surprised by his visit. He sat in a chair in front of my desk and came right out and told me that the board had made a mistake by letting me go; the new guy had bled the company of hundreds of thousands, the company was in trouble, had written only a handful of policies in the last two years, had no sales force, and needed me to come back and fix it. He told me I could name my own salary. I didn't know what to say. I had always fantasized about something like this happening, but I never thought it would. Yet here he was, offering me whatever I wanted. I told him that I now had started a small agency, and asked what I would I do with it. He said the company would buy it. This was getting better and better.

I leaned back in my chair and tried to digest what was happening. I won't lie: I was hurting for money, and naming my own salary was like something you only see in a movie. But did I want to sell out my principles again? As I sat there, I was thinking, *this is one of the guys who very hurtfully voted me out two years ago because they thought they could do it better. Now he's got the balls to sit here and ask me to come back and fix their mistakes, and he doesn't even have the good sense to apologize to me.* I leaned toward him and, after a calculated pause, told him no. I explained that regardless of what promises the board made, if I came back, after three months it would be the same old thing all over again, because if I was going to run a company and build it, I would have to do it my way, and there were too many different opinions of how things should be done. Plus, I told him I didn't trust them. He tried to convince me to change my mind, but I was firm in my decision. He left very disappointed. After he was gone, I let out a scream of victory.

Anybody who knew me knew I ate lunch in the same restaurant every day. It was no secret. The following week, another board member, George, "just happened to be passing by," and "accidentally" ran into me in the restaurant. He asked if he could join me. I said, "Sure." George was one of the two men who had lobbied the other board members to vote me off. He told me that he was running the company at the moment, but admitted he didn't know what he was doing and needed help. He, too, asked if I would come back and run the company and fix things. He, too, said I could name my salary. For me, two opportunities in one lifetime to strike back at my old "friends" were too good to be true. I pretended to think for a moment, and then had the great pleasure of telling him no. He understood, accepted my answer, and then was man enough to apologize for all the troubles he'd helped to cause me. He admitted that he and the board had been very wrong in their thinking, and it was the biggest mistake they could ever make, especially since my replacement had bilked them out of hundreds of thousands of dollars.

I was moved by his apology because I knew it was sincere, and I had been unconsciously waiting to hear it for over two years, but again, I told him no. We made small talk as we ate our lunch, and then he came up with an idea. He asked me if I would at least come in as a consultant to help him get on his feet, and train people in how to sell, so the Oak Lawn Company would have production again. This was too good to be true. My agency was hurting, and I was badly in need of money. Here was an opportunity to make things better without selling my soul. I would look at his company as an account for my agency, and

I would go there to service my account. They would pay my agency for the use of me. I agreed, and went there two mornings a week, nine till noon, helped them wherever I could, taught as many agents how to sell as they could bring to me, and for this service my agency received $400 a week. It was a win-win situation. In 1978, $400 a week was a lot of money, and I only worked six hours for it. The arrangement lasted for a year. My agency got healthy, and the Oak Lawn Company again had an agency force with steady production. They never gained the momentum we'd had in the beginning, but they continued for several years before they finally sold. The company is still in existence today, and George and I are friends to this day. In 1979, I married my wife Catherine.

If It Ain't Broke, Don't Fix It

I have related my experiences in detail. They are real, and they happened just as described. I know I am not unique, because this type of thing happens in one form or another, at one level or another, in companies all across America. It's better known as office or corporate politics. Like real politics, it can be rough, sometimes dirty, and almost always negative.

It doesn't have to be this way. If you are a manager or leader of some type, with people working under you, don't be afraid if one or more of them want your job. Encourage it. Teach them all that you can, and offer to help them grow. If everyone under you wants your job, that means they have to work for it. If they are working for it, that means productivity is up. And if your staff is doing a good job, that's a reflection on you. People above you will notice and know that you must be a good leader and are doing a good job. You will be noticed, and you will stand out. This could ultimately lead to a promotion, so you should be looking for ambition from your subordinates as a positive thing, not as a threat or a negative.

Motivation starts with management. If management is motivated, it will become contagious and spread to the people under you. People in management must know their jobs well, but the most successful managers are those who inspire and lead. A good manager does not just sit behind his desk shouting orders, but instead is not afraid to roll up his sleeves and work alongside his people. When people see you leading, they will work that much harder for you, and many times will go beyond the call of duty for you.

When working together as a team, people can accomplish more than they could if they were working as individuals. You can relate this to the story of the bundle of sticks. You can easily break an individual stick in two, but if you tie several sticks together in a bundle, and then try to break them, you will find it almost impossible. The point is that when people work together as a team, they are much stronger and will accomplish more than if each person was going his or her own way.

If you are in management, lead and work with your people as a team and your results will be tremendous. General George Patton was the most popular general in World War II. His troops not only loved him, but also were prepared to go that extra mile fighting the enemy. One reason for this was because Patton didn't stand behind the lines and dictate. He was out there leading his troops, riding into battle right alongside them. Because of the loyalty of his troops, Patton never lost a battle.

If more managers would view things in this manner, the companies they work for would grow more rapidly and, of course, have greater success. The more successful your company becomes, the better your chances of climbing the ladder to a higher position and, for sure, more money. Don't be afraid to give compliments for a job well done. We all need to hear that we are doing a good job. When we hear it, it energizes us. So, instead of getting fearful when someone under you is looking good, give that man or woman a pat on the back.

People work for money because it's a necessity of life. As much as money motivates people, recognition is an even better motivator. People will work harder when they feel appreciated and recognized. That pat on the back can be so important. Time after time, I have seen people work harder, give it their all, and give that extra push, just to get a trophy or to have their names on a plaque.

If you are a leader of a company, and your company is prospering because you have a good staff of hardworking people, and what you are doing is a winning formula, don't feel that you have to tweak it to make it better. Don't start fumbling around with changes. When a company has momentum, and it's growing, the slightest change or adjustment could have a negative effect that could domino and slow production. Once you lose momentum, it's very hard to restore it. If you have a winning formula, be happy. If it ain't broke, don't fix it.

We see things like this happen in companies more often than you think. People are creatures of habit. Sometimes the slightest change can cause an adverse effect. Take, for example, a successful TV show. The network will, for whatever reason, change its time slot. Suddenly the ratings drop because people no longer tune in. A show may change one of its main actors for some reason. Then viewership drops off, because people get used to one thing, and when change comes about, people change too.

What Do They Do?

If you are an individual working for a company, the pendulum can swing both ways. A pitfall that's easy to fall into is having the foolish thought that the person above you doesn't do anything. It's human nature to begin to believe you are doing all the work and the people above you aren't doing their fair share. Don't believe it. To be sure, there are some inept bosses and managers out there, but the bulk of management people have earned their positions because they have performed and are the right people for the job. Just remember, there is a flipside to that type of thinking. If you think the people above you don't do anything, then its fair to believe that the people under you think that you don't do anything either.

Again, if you are an individual working for a company, even at the lowest level, your job is to do the best that you can do, each and every day, and excel in your position. So go to work each day, stay positive, keep negative thoughts out of your mind, set goals for yourself pertaining to your job, and do your best to reach them. Don't let yourself be intimidated by your bosses, managers, or coworkers. You must know that you are good, and you must believe in yourself. For some reason or another, many people who may be well qualified never seem to climb above their current level. They never want to make decisions because they have a fear of being wrong and think they may be ridiculed. If this is how you feel, then you will never really accomplish anything worthwhile. Stick your neck out, make some decisions, and you might surprise yourself as to what you can achieve. People will have more respect for you if you are out there trying, and that includes your boss or supervisor. Yes, you may make a wrong decision or a wrong suggestion, but it might also be the right one. Either way, people will know that you are always thinking and always trying. You will be noticed. You may even get a promotion or a raise for your efforts.

Chapter seven

It Can't Be Done

Previously we talked about negatives, thinking positive, and deciding that you are going to do it. There is another element in the mix that you will hear about out there, especially if you are attempting to accomplish something that's either never been done before or is extremely hard to do. What you are going to hear is "You can't do it" or "That can't be done" or "It's impossible." The people who are making these statements are not telling you a lie. They really believe that it can't be done. Because they really do believe what they are saying, I don't classify what they say as a negative. It only becomes a negative if you start to believe what they are saying.

If you want to accomplish something that others say can't be done, you will have to be ignorant of the fact that it can't be done, and just do it.

Good Thing They Didn't Know

- ◆ Throughout history people have always said that something couldn't be done, but there were always those who didn't know it, and did it anyway. People used to say that man could never fly. Fortunately, the Wright Brothers didn't know that, and went ahead and invented the airplane. When Marconi, who invented the radio, told people he was going to send signals carrying the human voice through the air, and people would hear them hundreds of miles away, his family wanted to commit him. Good thing he didn't know that he couldn't do it. Beethoven, the great composer, was deaf.

- According to all the laws of aeronautics, the bumblebee can't fly. His body is too big and too heavy for its wingspan, and therefore can't lift off the ground. However, no one told the bumblebee. He doesn't know he can't fly, so he flies.

- After the Great Chicago Fire of 1871, hundreds of people, many of them businessmen, fled the city, never to return, because they said Chicago could never be rebuilt. This is understandable because the fire destroyed about 80 percent of the city. The flames consumed seventy-three miles of streets and 17,500 buildings, and killed about 300 people. It certainly appeared that everything was lost and the city could never rebuild. The fire started on a Sunday evening at 8:45 p.m., burned all the next day, and continued until 11:00 p.m. Monday, when it began to rain. The last of the flames were finally put out about 11:00 a.m. Tuesday. That afternoon, wagonloads of lumber were entering the city for the purpose of rebuilding. The people who ordered the lumber never got the message — they didn't know they couldn't rebuild. I was in downtown Chicago recently. They did a good job. The businessmen who left the city lost out; those who stayed enjoyed a windfall of business. Twenty-two years later, the city hosted the World's Columbian

Exposition (also known as The Chicago World's Fair), which 21 million people attended.

◆ Throughout the years there have been people from all walks of life who at sometime or other were told they couldn't do something. Sheer desire and a belief in themselves, plus the willpower to stay at it, have made many a man and woman successful and wealthy, and even heroes. There have been injured athletes who were told by doctors that they would never play again, only to come back and win marathons, bicycle races, championship football games, and Super Bowls. In the 1990s, Jim Abbott, who had only one hand, was a winning pitcher in major-league baseball, and Pete Gray, an outfielder for the St. Louis Browns in 1945, had only one arm.

◆ People who had paralysis of the arms and legs have become artists, holding the paintbrushes between their teeth, and creating beautiful paintings that have sold for large amounts of money.

◆ When our soldiers were trapped at the Battle of the Bulge during World War II, the Allied High Command determined that because of the distance, the terrain, and the very bad weather, it would take as long as a week to get reinforcements in to save them. By then it might have been too late. General George Patton said he could have his troops at Bastogne within forty-eight hours. The High Command said it was impossible. Forty-eight hours later Patton's troops were there, saving the day, Patton leading the way.

◆ One of the most moving examples of not knowing that something can't be done is the example of the baby. Imagine placing a toddler at one end of the room, and at the other end of the room lay a shiny metal object on the floor. The baby sees the object, and the only thing he knows is that he wants it. He can't quite walk yet, and still has a hard time crawling. He doesn't know that he can't get to the shiny metal object. Watch him as he crawls a few inches, and then tries to stand up. He takes a small step and then falls to the side. Remember the example for reaching goals. Remember the diagonal line. As you climb that line on your way to your goal at Point Z, you may stray off the line and fall to the side. The goal for the baby is the shiny object. He falls off course, but because he has no fear and no knowledge that it can't be done, he gets up again, wobbles, and takes another baby step. He may fall again, but the only thing he knows is that he wants that shiny object. Watch him as he falls and gets up over and over again, each time getting a little closer to his goal. If you let him be, he will gradually get there, no matter how long it takes. He never gives up, because he doesn't know what giving up is. He falls, goes off course, gets back on course, falls again, crawls a foot, gets up, takes a step, etc. Before long he will reach his goal, because he has no negatives in his head, because he doesn't understand the meaning of "can't." When he is about to retrieve the object, you can pick it up and set it on the sofa, and he still won't give up. He will crawl to the sofa, put his hands on the seat, and lift himself up so that he can reach across and get the object. As long as be sees what be wants, and believes he can get it, there will be no stopping him. If all adults would take this lesson from the baby, set a goal, and never give up, there would a lot more millionaires in this world today.

◆ There will always be people who will say it can't be done. These are usually people that don't amount to much when compared to the movers and shakers. Their attitude separates the successful people from the unsuccessful. There will always be new thoughts and new ideas, and there will always be people who don't know they can't do it, and proceed to do it anyway. There will always be people who have dreams, and fulfill those dreams because they just go after their goal and never quit until they have reached it.

◆ In 1893, many new inventions and ideas where introduced at the World's Columbian Exposition. Among the items were the Ferris wheel, the zipper, moving pictures, electric kitchen appliances, the X-ray machine, faucets, and new foods: Cracker Jack, Shredded Wheat, Juicy Fruit Gum, and Aunt Jemima's Pancake Mix. Despite all these innovations, there were people who believed that nothing new could be accomplished. Around the year 1900, a bill was introduced in Congress proposing to close down the U.S. Patent Office because there was nothing left to invent. If you could go back to 1900 and tell people of what life is like today, with the airplane, TV, computers, the Internet, cell phones, antibiotics, and all the thousands of inventions we take for granted, they wouldn't believe it, and would tell you, "It can't be done." The creators of all of those inventions over the last century surely never knew that they couldn't do it.

Raising 2 Million Dollars

Earlier I told you of how, in 1973, I started the Oak Lawn life insurance company. I had previously learned that at that time, a person could form a company in Illinois with up to twenty-five investors, or incorporators, with no need to do filings with the state of Illinois. I also knew that to start a life insurance company in Illinois, you needed $2 million, half of which would be deposited with the state before you received the license, or charter, to do business. I decided to start with twenty-five people, myself included, form a base, then file, and go public with a stock sale.

I picked $15,000 as the amount to be invested by each of the twenty-five, which would give me a base of $375,000. The remainder of the money would be raised from the public stock sale. I did not have $15,000. I had recently come out of a divorce and was doing all I could to stay above water. I went to two different banks, explained what I was going to do, and asked for a loan of $15,000 on my name alone, since I no longer owned any property. After the bankers stopped laughing, they of course turned me down. To them I was just a young man with no collateral who was setting out to do something that could not be done. Looking back I can understand how they felt. To them, I was a stranger looking for $15,000, which in 1973 was a considerable amount, and the idea of raising $2 million had to sound really farfetched to them. As for me, I never saw it as a problem. I never thought I couldn't do it, nor did I think it would be hard.

After being turned down twice, without the bankers believing in even the slightest that I could deliver, I decided to go a different route. I went to a bank in Alsip, Illinois, and told the banker of my plans. I left out the part about my needing a loan. I did, however, tell him that I would get each of twenty-five investors to put $15,000 into his bank. This made him happy, because every banker wants new deposits in his bank, and I was talking a lot of money. I knew that he, like the others, didn't believe me, because after all, I had come in off the street talking about a crazy idea of raising $2 million, but what did he have to lose? You can also be sure that he figured I would never get the two million, and that it would take me months to get the twenty-five depositors, if I could get them at all.

I had already consulted with a downtown Chicago attorney who specialized in setting up corporations and stock sales. He advised me how to bring in the twenty-five investors in a way that their money would be protected in case I failed to put my base together. I never doubted I would get the base together, but the method I used did give everyone peace of mind. After I had the bank in place, I started calling on businessmen I knew, and whom I knew had the money. Once they were onboard, I would ask them to find someone they knew, and bring him in, and in turn asked that person to find someone he knew.

The third day after I had set up with the bank, I met the first investor there. In fact, I met every investor at the bank. Each investor would open up a $15,000 CD in his own name, and sign a letter of direction to the bank stating that when I had twenty-five such letters, his CD money could be transferred to the corporate account. When that occurred, all the investors would then be called incorporators.

The banker was astonished. He saw me every day, and sometimes twice a day, with a new depositor. The whole effort took three weeks. By the end of the third week, the banker was giving me the red carpet treatment. I made a believer out of him, and he could now see and taste the $2 million. I sat down at his desk, and handed him twenty-four letters of direction, representing $360,000. Then I told him the twenty-fifth investor was myself, and broke the news that I needed a loan of $15,000. Fifteen minutes later the corporate account had $375,000 in it.

It was now time to go public with the stock sale. For this, you need a prospectus, a legal booklet-type document that describes in detail the type and scope of the corporation, its purpose and goals, and full details of the officers and other people involved.

You cannot sell stock without a prospectus, and your prospectus must be filed and approved by the Office of the Secretary of State's Securities Division. Everyone who buys the stock receives a prospectus, and is supposed to read it first. We had all the stockholders sign a form saying that they had received a prospectus.

I went back to the lawyer with two men who were going to help run the company with me. They were Bill and Lynn, both previously with the Decatur Company, working under me in my territory. It was a Friday. For the past few weeks, the attorney had worked at writing the prospectus, completed it, and had preliminary copies ready to be filed for approval by the Secretary of State. That afternoon the attorney was going to send them to Springfield, along with the proper forms for filing. We were very anxious to get started selling the stock because neither Bill nor Lynn nor I had any income, and we wouldn't have any until we had started the insurance company and could sell insurance. We were thinking that in a couple of weeks we would be able to start selling stock so we could get the insurance company funded and could be in business. Then our attorney dropped a bombshell on us.

He didn't know that we were unaware that getting a prospectus approved by the state would take six months minimum, and maybe a year. We felt like our legs had been cut off. He assured us that this was his business, that he had handled many such filings, and six months was a normal wait time — it was impossible to do it any sooner. As far as we were concerned, this was unsatisfactory. We needed it now, and, against his advice, we took matters into our own hands. Even though he said we were making a big mistake, we took our prospectus and all the paperwork that needed to be filed with the State, and left his office.

We didn't know how it would work out, but we took a shot at

getting the prospectus approved ourselves. Bill left for Springfield early Monday morning. He arrived at the Secretary of State's office at 9:00 a.m. He walked up to the desk and handed the packet to the man in charge of securities. Bill told him he was filing for approval, and if they could look it over and approve it, he would wait. I wasn't there, but I am sure this brought a chuckle to the man in charge. He told Bill not to wait because it would take quite some time. Bill told him he was staying at a local motel, and would be back later in the day. The securities office closed at 4:00 p.m., and Bill came back before closing only to find that the packet was still sitting where he had left it on the desk.

At 9:00 the next morning, Bill was again standing before the securities man's desk. The guy looked a little irritated. Bill hung around the office all day, except when he went to lunch, and waited in plain sight of the people in charge. This must have irritated them even more, and they must have figured they had to get rid of this guy, so that day the man in charge gave the prospectus to someone to look at. Shortly before 4:00 o'clock, he handed the prospectus back to Bill for corrections. Almost every page had been marked in red ink changing this or changing that. I'm sure their thought was that Bill would now have to go back to Chicago, go to the printer, and have it revised, that this would take considerable time, and Bill would be out of their hair for a while. Boy, were they in for a shock.

Bill went back to his motel room and called me at our Oak Lawn office where I was waiting for his call. With my copy of the prospectus in front of me, we went through it page by page, with me marking the corrections on my copy. When we finished, I called the printer. We were working with a really good firm located in downtown Chicago. They specialized in printing legal documents like the prospectus, and they were open around the clock. With his copy in front of him, I fed him all the corrections. When we finished, he said he would go to press immediately. Shortly before midnight, Lynn and I arrived at the printer's, picked up the corrected copies, and then turned the car toward Springfield. We met with Bill at 3:00 a.m., gave him the corrected copies, then turned around and drove back home. You must remember that in 1973 there was no email, no personal computers, no fax machines, or other electronic devices for sending data instantly.

I wish I could have been there the next morning just to see the look on the securities man's face. Bill described it for me. It was Wednesday morning. Bill announced to him that he had the corrected copy, and asked him to please review and approve it. The man's jaw almost hit the floor. He couldn't believe what he was hearing. How could anybody move that fast? He gave the copy to the person who had reviewed it the day before. Again, Bill hung around in plain sight the rest of the day. At closing time, the copy, with a new set of corrections marked in red, was handed to Bill. This time there were fewer corrections than the first time. Bill went back to the motel, called me, and I called the printer. Lynn and I picked up the new copy at midnight, and delivered it to Bill in Springfield at 3:00 a.m.

On Thursday morning, the securities department had a new corrected copy to review. The people in charge were absolutely dumbfounded, and were a bit annoyed at the persistence shown by Bill and his company. Four o'clock came, and again the copy was returned to Bill, this time with just a few corrections. Bill called me, I called the printer, and we made yet another run to Springfield.

On Friday morning Bill was there again with the corrected copy. According to Bill, the securities man was now so aggra-vated he grabbed the copy, never looked it over, pulled out all the forms, stamped everything approved, and asked Bill to get the hell out. We had done it! In fact we put a big sign in our window at the Oak Lawn office that said, "WE DID IT." People on the street didn't know what we did, but it was fun anyway, and a very proud moment for us. Then came more fun. After Bill called me that morning to tell me our prospectus was approved and he was on his way back home, I had the privilege of calling our attorney to ask if he remembered the prospectus that he had said, just seven days ago, would take a minimum of six months to get approved, and that we were making a big mistake. I told him we had gotten it approved. There was a long silence at his end of the line. I am sure that his whole career was going through his mind, trying to figure out where he'd gone wrong. However, he really was a good attorney, and because we all liked him very much, we didn't needle him about it. A week later, we were selling stock to the public.

To sell the stock, we used the dinner-meeting concept that had always worked so well, except there were no dinners this time, just coffee or soda. We used one restaurant exclusively, because it was conveniently located, the owner was one of the incorporators, and he made sure our meeting room was always undisturbed. We started by asking all of the twenty-five incorporators to come to our first meeting with at least two or three friends, and then we would ask those people to bring their friends to the next meeting, etc. I gave all the presentations, which lasted only about thirty minutes. At every meeting we had a table set up in the corner of the room, with three ladies sitting there to take stock orders and pick up checks. Before the presentation we passed out forms for the prospects to complete with their personal information if they wanted to purchase stock. The stock sold for $3 per share, with a minimum of one hundred shares. After each presentation was finished, I would ask those who might be interested in purchasing stock to form three single lines at the table, have their checkbooks out, and tell the ladies how much stock they wished to purchase. It never failed. We always had three single lines, and picked up, on average, between $20,000 and $30,000 per meeting. We held two to three meetings each week.

At our very last meeting, something strange happened, or so I thought at the time. At each meeting, we averaged thirty to forty attendees. The final meeting we held was advertised as the last, and we had almost one hundred people attend. About ten minutes into my presentation, I announced that this would be the last meeting, because we were shutting the stock sale down, even though everyone there knew it. Suddenly, it seemed like the whole room stood up and started heading for the door. I was dumbfounded. I didn't know what I had said that would make everybody want to leave. Then I noticed that at this particular meeting, the ladies had set up the table in front of the door, and instead of leaving, the people were forming three long lines to buy our stock. They just wanted to be sure they got some. I never did finish that presentation. We picked up close to $200,000 that night.

Altogether, we sold $1,750,000 worth of stock. From start to finish, it took four months to the day. It was unbelievable. A week later we gave the State of Illinois $1 million, received our charter to do business as a life insurance company, and commenced business about a week later. Throughout the entire experience of raising money, from the initial $375,000 to the additional $1,750,000, I never heard anyone say to me, "It can't be done," except for our lawyer who said we couldn't get the prospectus approved in less than six months. We never believed him anyway — you know how lawyers lie. I expect that the reason I never had any negative comments was because most of the people knew me from my Decatur Company experience, had seen firsthand my confidence and abilities, and knew I could build a company. What I did get, however, after we were done, were comments from others asking, "How did you do that?" It turns out that 1973 was a recession year. Gas prices and unemployment were up, and things were tough all over. I didn't know that, and neither did Bill or Lynn. We were so busy working night and day we never paid attention to TV or the news. We just went out and did our job, then found out it was impossible to do. Good thing nobody had told us.

Summary

I read once that if you tell a man there are 200 billion stars in the universe, he will believe you, but if you tell him a bench has just been painted, he has to touch it to make sure. Why do some people, when told that they can't do something, automatically accept the statement as true, and never pursue what they were trying to accomplish? Why can't they be suspicious and touch it to make sure? Just because someone tells you something, don't immediately accept it as truth. Give it your own test for truthfulness.

The world is filled with people who have never fulfilled their real potential because somewhere along the way they listened to the negatives and to the people who said, "It can't be done." The world is full of people who say, "If only" or "I wish I had" or any of a thousand statements people come up with to justify their positions in their careers or in their lives. *People don't plan to fail — they just fail to plan.* Many of those who do plan don't have the stamina to stay with their plan until it becomes reality. Nobody ever said getting where you want to go would be easy, but they have said, "You can't get there." Look at your life as it is today. Are you happy with yourself? Are you satisfied that you are all you can be? If you answer no to these questions, then sit down and review your life. Figure out where you want to be. Make a plan, set a goal, and go for it. You might not reach it, but in the process you will have grown to levels you would have never thought possible for yourself.

Look at your goal as being at the top of a staircase, and you are at the bottom of the staircase. Don't just stand there. Take that first step, and then keep on climbing. If you keep on going you will reach the top. Even if you don't make it to the top of the staircase, you will have climbed to greater heights. If you keep moving you will, if I may use the word, "stumble" onto something good, maybe when you least expect it. No one ever stumbled onto something good while sitting down.

Chapter eight

Helping the Competition

In the classic movie *Miracle on 34th Street,* Kris Kringle takes a job as a Santa for Macy's department store. As the children come to see him with their Christmas wish lists, some ask for items Macy's doesn't carry. Kris, looking out for the children's interests, advises the parents to go to a competing store because they carry the items. When the manager hears this, he is shocked, and fearful that he will lose his job as head of the toy department. His coworker fires Kris, but they have to quickly hire him back because Mr. Macy calls both of them into his office to let them know how happy he is. He thinks it was their idea to send customers to a competitor, and he's being flooded with letters and phone calls from customers who are grateful that Macy's has adopted the policy of recommending other stores that carry the items they're looking for. The goodwill this gesture creates is invaluable, and Macy's business grows by leaps and bounds.

Miracle on 34th Street is a wonderful story. I don't suggest that you tell everyone to go buy your product or service from someone else; but if you plan to be in business to stay, it's good business to look for what's best for your customers. If you know that your product is not the best for their particular needs, then be honest with them, and steer them to what would be better.

This gesture takes a big person, but the goodwill you will create is as valuable as the goodwill Macy's experienced in the movie. Your clients will sincerely appreciate your honesty. They will recommend you to their friends. They may also surprise you and convince themselves that your product or service might be best for them after all. No one likes a pushy salesperson, and the fact that you didn't try to twist their arms, but instead looked out for them, will make you a standout person in their eyes. Word will get around about your character, your professionalism, and your honesty.

In my business, there have been many occasions over the years when I would review policies that clients purchased elsewhere. After reviewing their policies, if I felt the coverage was good and the price they were paying was fair, and if I thought changing over to me would not gain them better coverage or any substantial savings, I would advise the clients to stay where they were, and keep their policies because they were good. I was always pleased with the look of gratitude I would see on their faces. At that very moment I would bond with them. And what would that honesty bring me? Business I would never have had. The clients I am speaking of would recommend me to all their friends and relatives. I would become the trusted insurance man, and usually, within a year or so, I would wind up insuring the clients anyway, because they realized that I would take better care of their needs and they would be happier with me as their insurance agent. In the end, the sales I turned away usually came back tenfold.

Don't Knock the Competition

Never put yourself in the position of badmouthing your competition to others. This will never help your stature as a businessperson; it is not professional, and certainly won't earn you points with anyone. When you run down the competition, you cheapen yourself and make yourself look small. Instead, when a client mentions a competitor to you, always praise the competitor as being a good person or company, but then tell your client the advantages of dealing with you, your product, and your service. In the end, you will stand out as the professional.

There is a good rule you can follow regarding your thoughts about the competition: *If you can't say anything good about a person or company, then don't say anything at all.*

You may find yourself in situations when you are the one who is being badmouthed by the competition. Clients might tell you that the other guy said this or said that about you or your product. This has happened to me on more than one occasion. I would look my client right square in the eye and assure him or her, "My product is good, I stand behind it, and I wouldn't steer you wrong." I would also explain that the person who talked negatively about me or my product was a good person, but he was misinformed or insecure, and they should ask him to put his comments in writing.

This, I promise you, will not happen. No one will ever put negative comments about someone else in writing. In the process, the client sees how professional you are, because you said your competitor was a good person, and you didn't stoop to his level of name-calling. Let the other guy do the name-calling. You make sure you keep your composure and your dignity.

A Real-life Example

In 1991, I had a home built for my family and myself. It was located on a new one-block area consisting of seventeen custom homes. We were the third family to move onto the block. It was spring, and weeds and mud were everywhere, and everyone's home needed landscaping. Someone recommended a man to me who was just starting out on his own. I could relate to him from the business point of view because I knew how hard starting a new business could be.

He was of Irish decent, and his name was Paddy. He was married, had six young children, and was struggling to make a name for himself. When Paddy stopped by my home to give me a bid, I assessed him as being honest and honorable. I will, however, confess that I was living in the past, maybe as far back as twenty years, as to the cost of landscaping. Once I got over my initial shock, I had to analyze just what I could afford to have done at that time.

Paddy also gave bids to a few other neighbors on the block. In the meantime, a second landscaper came through giving bids, and he was badmouthing Paddy. He told people they would be making a big mistake to hire Paddy because he would start a job, take the money, and then never come back to finish. Maybe because of my experiences in the business world, where hurtful rumors were spread about me, I was immediately suspicious of this second landscaper. I don't like when businessmen badmouth other businessmen, but some of the neighbors did buy his story, and hired him. When he came back to do the landscaping for them, he did a good job, and his work was professional, but to me that wasn't the point.

About two weeks later Paddy stopped by our house to see if we had made a decision. We sat around our kitchen table and he outlined a plan for my yard with a little less work than we originally talked about, and a price that I could handle. I liked him, and I gave him the go-ahead to do the work. After I committed myself, he asked me if I knew what the neighbors were doing, because he hadn't heard back from any of them. At first I was reluctant to say, because I really didn't know what certain neighbors had decided, or why, and because I don't like to criticize anyone. Paddy could see I was holding back, so he pressed me for an answer. Finally, I had to tell him what the rumor was and who was spreading it. Paddy was shocked and a bit angered, but he assured me the rumors were unfounded. I assured him that I hadn't bought into the rumors to begin with, that I felt comfortable with him, and that was why I had hired him.

Paddy was scheduled to start my yard one week later. He must have been festering over the bad rap he was getting, because he called me three times during that week. In the first call, he asked if I would mind if he could add a couple of features to my landscaping plan, and I told him I was okay with it. In the second call, he asked if he could be more artistic. Again, I said yes. On his third call, he asked me right out if he could have carte blanche. By this time I didn't care anymore, and I told him to do whatever he felt he needed to do. I figured I would find a way to pay for it. Besides, I had a feeling something good was coming.

Paddy made it his goal to give me the best yard he could ever do, and to be sure, the best on the block. When he arrived with his trucks loaded with sod, shrubs, trees, and bushes, my jaw dropped. On top of all that, he brought in paver bricks. It was a spectacle to behold. He decided he was going to show everyone on the block that he was the best, and in the process make my yard a showplace. He did exactly that, and it cost me far less than if I had ordered it to begin with. My backyard looks like a park. I not only believe I have the most beautiful yard on the block, but the most beautiful yard in all of Cook County, Illinois. Then again, I'm biased. I show it off to as many people as I can, because my wife and I are proud of it, and we let Paddy send his prospective clients over to see it as often as he wants to.

I tell this story because it is a living example of what bad-mouthing the competition can do. When you criticize, you lose. The other landscaper cheapened himself in my eyes, and Paddy came out the true professional for everyone to see. As far as his reputation for being honest and honorable, and for the quality of his work, Paddy's future success started with my yard.

Working with the Competition

Good businesspeople tend to find each other as they are climbing their success ladders. Make it a point to meet and get to know your competitors. Become friends with them. Compare notes with them. Offer your help if they need anything. Share good advice with them, and teach them how to do better if you can. This type of goodwill can only serve to make all of you more successful. The door swings both ways. You may need their help at some point. If you give of yourself generously, you will receive generously in return. Also, if you are all friends helping each other, no one will be badmouthing anybody else.

In my business, I know many of my competitors, and we help each other. Whatever business you are in, you may not always be able to fill the customer's needs, but maybe your competition can, so you help each other in this way. You send him a client, and he may send you a client when he can't fill his customer's needs.

When I first opened my insurance agency I was struggling and hurting for money. To pick up some extra cash, I took a job one night a week teaching insurance licensing at the local community college. I taught three classes per year, and on average there were twenty-five people in each class. This meant that each year I was putting seventy-five potential competitors into my field of business. Someone asked me why I would want to do this. Why would I want all this competition? I never had any concerns whatsoever. Today, because of my class, there are several people selling insurance and a couple of successful agencies, but we are all friends and we help each other.

The truth is, my agency grew because I was teaching people my business. Even though people went to the school, it doesn't mean they followed up, got their licenses, and went into business. The great majority did not. But in the process, I got to know them and they got to know me. Many households knew my name. Many of these people became clients and bought their insurance from me. Many of them sent their friends and relatives to me for insurance. Teaching helped my agency grow and prosper. If you ever have the chance to teach your trade or profession, do it. You will not only be helping others, you will also be helping yourself. By the way, if you really want to learn your trade or profession, try teaching it. You will be amazed at how much more you'll learn.

I originally planned to teach at the college for one year. Long after the point of needing the money, I continued teaching because, to be honest, I liked it, I was having fun, and I knew each class meant a new batch of future policies. I taught insurance at the college for twelve years.

Chapter nine

The Arts of Selling

So FAR WE have discussed success, having knowledge, fighting negativity, staying positive and enthused, belief in yourself, and setting goals and deciding you are going to achieve them. All of the above are meaningless unless you actually get into the trenches, roll up your sleeves, and get to work. Now we get down to the nitty-gritty of meeting the client face to face, eyeball to eyeball, and making the sale of your product or service.

In this chapter I will take you step by step from prospecting for clients to closing the sale. I will talk to you about the techniques and fundamentals of selling as I learned and practiced them. I will not discuss anything that I haven't done myself. These are the same techniques and basics that I have taught to hundreds of people over the years. Unfortunately, much of this knowledge is slowly becoming lost in this age of computers and on-line selling. People are just not being trained today in the proven methods that have made many a salesperson successful, and there are those who say there is no need to be trained because of new technologies. I don't agree. Just like you learn to crawl before you walk, you should learn the basics if you are going to be successful. Technology cannot and will not do it all, and there will be times in your career when knowledge of the fundamentals of selling becomes extremely important. I am not saying that no companies teach these basic concepts, but the new technology is taking over. I don't condemn the new technology, but if you are starting out on a new career or business venture, nothing works better than the old-fashioned method of "See the people, see the people, see the people."

Prospecting — Making a List

You just finished your initial training in your chosen profession, whether you are selling insurance, vacuum cleaners, Avon products, or building a hairdressing business. Where do you start? First, you have to let everyone you know, and the people you will meet in the future, what you do. You have to get the word out. I don't mean that you run to people and ask them to buy. You let everyone know in a casual way what you are doing, and you ask him or her to think of you the next time they are in the market for your product or service. In this way, they will not feel pressured, and they will be more relaxed when they see you in the future. Never let them see you sweat. Never let them think you are desperate to make a sale. Always have the air about you that you are doing well. Knowing that you are not being pushy with them will allow them to comfortably ease their way to you when they are looking for your product or service. The more people you let know, the larger the clientele you will build. It seems like when the first few trickle your way, the rest start to follow more rapidly.

Who are these people you will be talking to? I can't stress this next statement enough: "MAKE A LIST." List everyone you know — your parents, your family, your friends, the guy at the gas station, the grocer, and the people you see in restaurants. Keep adding to your list as you keep thinking of people. Keep paper and pen on your nightstand. When you wake up in the middle of the night and remember someone's name, write it down then and there. If you wait until morning, you will forget whom you were thinking about.

Your list should never be completed, because you will continue to think of new people, and if you are out working, you will continue to meet new ones. Once you begin your list, start working it. Check off each name as you see them and let them know what you are doing.

The beginning of your career may not be the only time you make a list. In business there are good spells and there are downturns, when things get slow. During a downturn, you may need to jumpstart yourself again by starting a new list. In my business, I have had good times and not-so-good times. In 1984, I had a severe downturn. I was writing very little business. I went back to the basics and put together a list of about one hundred people. I phoned the first two, but there was no answer. I called the third person on my list, a doctor, found that he was home, and made an appointment for the next evening. I went to that man's home, and in one night, in one sitting, sold enough life insurance to make commissions totaling $36,000. The insurance company I placed the business with gave me a $10,000 bonus and an all-expense-paid trip to Maui for my wife and myself. In sales, you always hear about, or you are told, the story of some guy who went out and made a sale worth thousands of dollars in one night. You always ask yourself if these people really exist. Suddenly, I was the guy. LISTS WORK!

When you are letting people know what you do, always ask them if they have friends or know of anyone who could use your product or service. Don't ever be afraid to ask. People will help you. The good doctor sent me to see a friend of his and I wrote enough life insurance to make another $15,000 in commissions.

Cold Calling by Phone

The most common fear salespeople have is phone fear. You may find yourself cold calling people whom you do not know and have not been referred to you. I won't say this is easy, but if you find that you have to do it, remember: the worst thing that can happen is the person on the other end of the line says no and hangs up. You didn't get physically hurt; your ego just got bruised a little. When calling someone you don't know and who was not a referral, you need a friendly way about you, and a winning personality. Don't use high pressure; instead, explain that you just want the opportunity to show him something he might like. When calling cold, be sure the person is not on the "DO NOT CALL" list.

It's a lot easier calling someone who has been referred to you, because you have a common thread. Both of you know the person who did the referring. A good tip to remember: never call people at the dinner hour, whether they are referrals or not.

Before you sit down to start your calls, psyche yourself up. Look in the mirror and tell yourself you are going to do it. Take a deep breath. Think happy, positive thoughts. Your positive attitude will be reflected on the other end of the line.

Monday evenings were my night to call people and set up appointments for the week. When I called, I would always give the impression that I was busy and had a lot of people to see. As I progressed to making an appointment with the client, I would look at my appointment calendar for the week, and it would, of course, be empty. However, I would tell my prospect that I had an opening tomorrow at 7:00, or Thursday at 8:00. I might also tell him that I might be able to squeeze him in on Wednesday if we could do it before 6:00. I would then ask which day would be best for him and his wife? This would always give the impression that I was busy seeing other clients who wanted my product. It would also say to him that I was successful. People want to deal with successful people. They do not want to feel like they are the only ones out there that you are calling.

At this time I need to point out to you that unless you are talking to a businessman at his place of business about a product that affects his business, all presentations affecting the family or household must be given when both husband and wife are present. Otherwise, you will hear, "That sounds good, but I really have to discuss it with my wife." When you present to one person, you are giving him (or her) a perfect way out; he will always tell you that he can't make the decision without first discussing it with his spouse, and it may be very hard for you to get a chance to come back.

Calling on Your Friends and Relatives

For many of the reasons I mentioned earlier, your friends and relatives may very well be the hardest people to sell your product or service to. However, you have to start somewhere, and at this point friends and relatives pretty much cover your circle of would-be clients. You must know that the word has already gone out through your entire family that you are doing something new and you may be calling on them to buy something. By now they have prepared themselves and thrown up defensive walls. So how do you get them to sit down with you and listen to your presentation?

The method I used when I first started selling insurance came to me from those three instructors at the school in Decatur. Your friends and relatives know that sooner or later you will be calling on them. They know that day is coming, and in some cases they are dreading it, because they have already made up their minds that they don't want to buy anything. Before you call on any of them, be sure you have your presentation down pat. Practice, practice, and practice, because when you do see your relatives, you want to be at your best. Look at yourself in the mirror and make the presentation to yourself.

When I felt I was ready, I would call on, let's say, my Uncle Harry. You want to call on the person who you think is the most influential in your family first. I would tell him I was sure by now that he'd heard, through the family, of the new field I was in, and about the product I was selling, which was life insurance. I would then proceed to tell him I didn't want to sell him anything, but that I needed his help before I started calling on real prospects. I needed for him to listen to my presentation, and when I finished, I wanted him to tell me how I had done. In fact, I wanted a report card from him. I have now taken Uncle Harry off the hook. He would feel relieved that I didn't want to sell him anything, and feel complimented that I thought so highly of his opinion as to want it. All of a sudden he would actually feel a little power. He would say, "Sure, come on out." Now I had to give the best presentation of my life. I had to be so good and so enthused that, when I was finished, he would say that he wanted one of those policies. I assured him that it was not my intention to sell him anything, and I really hadn't come there to take his money. However, in the process, I made him feel like *he* had discovered something good, and now he wanted it.

After making the sale I would ask for his help again. I would ask whether he knew anyone whom he thought would like this policy, and to please recommend me to him or her. You should do this after every sale — always ask for referrals. If you ask, people will help you. Another plus about talking to Uncle Harry first was that he would now tell the rest of the family to see me because I had something good and they should get involved with it. Coming from Uncle Harry, this was the best endorsement I could possibly get as far as family was concerned. If Uncle Harry had a policy, they wanted one.

To approach family, I can't think of a better way than this "back door method." I never made anyone feel pressured; I even balked when he or she wanted to buy. I took them all off the hook as far as buying anything, and instead complimented them by seeking their opinions. This approach will work on family and friends regardless of what you are selling, whether it's insurance, vacuum cleaners, book club memberships, or almost any other product.

Cold Calling in Person

If you are selling a product that is primarily for businesses, in my case it was business insurance, you may want to cold call in person. My technique for this was to pick a business area, then walk down the street and stop at every business along the way. I would never walk into a business and ask them to buy. My approach was simple: I would walk in and ask for the manager or owner. I would then apologize for interrupting what ever he was doing, and explain that I just wanted to say hello and give him my card. I would always acknowledge that I was sure he was properly insured, but that when he had a chance he should give me a call, because I might be able to save him money. No one will ever get mad at you because you want to help him or her save money. The whole approach would take less than three minutes. I would thank him for his time, then turn and walk out. There was never any high pressure on my part, so he would feel off the hook. You would be surprised how many businessmen would stop me as I was leaving and want to talk right then and there. If I insured other businesses in the area, I would always mention their names. Once I dropped a familiar business name to them, they would want to talk to me all the more.

There is another exercise I would do. Each weekday morning, I would leave the house early, go into a restaurant, and buy a cup of coffee. I would be sure to exchange some type of small talk with the waitress and the regulars who were there, and then I would leave. My next stop was the next restaurant. I would have another coffee, make more small talk, and leave. I would visit the same two or three restaurants each morning. After a while everyone knew me and was happy to see me, always saying hello or good morning. Eventually, someone would ask what I did for a living, and I would tell him or her. I would never ask anybody to buy, but I would ask that they remember me when they were in the market or when their renewal came up, because I might be able to save them money. In the end, I always became the resident insurance man of the restaurant.

Mailings

Another technique for building clientele is mass mailings. This will work better for some businesses than for others. It all depends on what product or service you are selling. I never really took to a mailing program. You can send out hundreds of letters, or postcards, or whatever type of brochure you might be using, but then you have to rely on the prospect calling you. With postage, this can get expensive, and you may not get the desired results.

When I used the mailing concept, I mailed out ten letters per day. After about a week, I would follow up and call the first ten to see if they would like to see me. Every day I would call the ten people I had mailed to a week ago. I saw some results, and maybe if I had worked it harder and longer I would have seen more, but I had other techniques that served me much better, so I concentrated more on those. I won't say you should never try a mailing campaign, because if you don't try, you will always wonder, but for me, it wasn't what worked best.

Buying Leads

There are companies that sell lists of what they call qualified leads for a variety of products and services including insurance. Supposedly, the people on these lists want your product or service and are waiting for someone to call them. Lists of leads can cost hundreds of dollars. I would advise you not to waste your money. I have tried this a couple of times, only to find that many of the people on the lists don't live there anymore, or the phone numbers have been disconnected, and if you do get hold of someone on the list, they either don't know what you're talking about or they're not interested. Before you spend your money on such a list, open the phone book. There are plenty of names in it, and the chances of selling to them are just as good as the ones on the lists.

Making the Presentation

You have made the appointment, and now you are in the client's home or place of business. If you are in the home, the preferable place is the kitchen table. I will explain later just how you can put yourself there. When you arrive, smile and keep smiling. If you are smiling, the client is smiling and is getting comfortable with you. Be enthusiastic. If you are enthused, friendly, and smiling, most of your work is already done, because the client will also smile, be friendly with you, and get enthused.

Depending on what type of product you are selling, you may present it to your client by using a presentation book, brochures, or the actual product itself. When giving your presentation, you will want to be sharp, enthusiastic, and always honest. You must know your product inside and out, and you must not only believe in it, but also be excited about it. Remember, it's hard to sell something that you wouldn't buy yourself. Always explain your product in a professional way. Be knowledgeable enough about your product that if the client asks you a question you can give him a crisp, solid answer. You don't want to stumble, fishing for an answer, and for sure, you do not want to make one up. If you don't know the answer, look the client in the eye, and compliment him on such an intelligent question. Tell him no one has ever asked you that before, and admit you don't know. Honesty is always important. The client might already know the answer and is just testing you. Assure him you will find out and let him know, then follow up and do it.

Have your materials in order when you are presenting. You want to be precise, clear, and to the point. You do not want to fumble through your paperwork or brochures, looking for information. Have your materials in order, and present them in the order that takes you through your presentation.

Give your presentation briefly and effectively. You don't want to run more than fifteen or twenty minutes because you may lose your client's attention. Do not talk too much. Explain the program, then shut up and go for the close. Many a salesman has talked too much, trying to impress the client, and talked himself right out of a sale.

The occasion might arise when you go on a joint call with another salesperson. I never found this desirable. In the event you do, remember this important advice: When two salespeople go on a call together, only one talks, and the other shuts up; he talks only if the client asks him a direct question, which he answers and then shuts up again. The reason I give this advice is because you must control the meeting. If two salespeople talk at the same time, the client will control the meeting, and chances are no sale will be made. Before you go in, decide which of you will do the talking. I once lost a big sale because I brought an overzealous salesman with me. He was so set on letting the client know how smart he was that he couldn't shut up, even though I was the one who was supposed to speak. He talked so much and gave the client so much information that the client figured out he really didn't need to buy after all — and he didn't.

Closing the Sale — Objections

To close means to make the sale. You made the appointment, you gave the presentation, and now it's time to close the deal. Ninety-five percent of closing the deal starts in your own mind. Your mind must be conditioned to know that you *are* going to make the sale; it's not a question of *if* you are going to make the sale. Remember, we talked about positive thinking, setting goals, and believing that you can do it. Your goal is to make the sale, and in your mind you have to know you are going to make the sale from the moment you set up the appointment. After the appointment is set, all you should have to do is show up, go through the ritual of explaining your product, and write the paperwork. If you leave your home to see the client with the frame of mind and belief I just explained, then 95 percent of your work is done. There are many different closing techniques. The following are the most common.

Give Him a Choice Close – When you are finished presenting your product, the next natural step is to write the paperwork. Everything should be a smooth, even flow. When you are finished presenting your product, take out the necessary forms and, with pen in hand, start filling them out by asking a closing question. For example:

"Are you going to be paying this in full, or would you like a payment plan?"

If there is an objection or a question, it will come now, and you will handle it. If you did your job well, and gave an enthusiastic presentation, five out of ten times, the client will answer your closing question and give you his preference of payment. Do the paperwork, take the check, thank your client, and leave.

I know that all of this sounds fairly easy. It really is, if you have confidence. You never want to ask your client if he or she wants to buy. You will be giving him a chance to say no. Believe me, clients want to buy. If they didn't, you would never have gotten the appointment. Subconsciously, people want to buy, but they need to feel that *they* found a good product, or *they* made a good deal. When you leave their home, they need to feel that *they* did the right thing. It's your job to make them feel this way. Whether they want to buy is not a question you want to ask. That question will only bring them back to the reality that you are there to try to sell them something. You must always assume that they are going to purchase your product or service. You have to know this from the moment you leave your house to drive there. You must ask questions that give the client a choice to make, and when he makes that choice, he has committed himself to buying your product.

Depending on what type of product or service you are selling, the questions will vary. Here are a few examples to help you open your mind and design questions that fit your particular product or service:

- Would you like the red one or the blue one?

- Would you like to pay annually or would you prefer monthly?

- Would you like to be billed on the first or the fifteenth of the month?

- Would you like the new curly style, or would you prefer to keep your hair straight?

- Would you like one box or three boxes for the price of two?

I could go on and on, but you can see the pattern. Always close with questions involving a choice for the client, a choice that commits him to buy. If the client has a question or an objection, he will bring it up then. When he does ask you a question, you compliment him for asking such an intelligent question, making him feel that you recognize he has a keen mind, and then you answer it clearly and professionally. Then you repeat the closing question with the choice again. Always look your client squarely in the eyes when you are doing this. It's hard for him to say no if he is looking right at you.

Objections may be thrown at you. The worst thing you can do is to be afraid of them. Know that there will be objections, and be prepared to answer them. The objections will vary, depending on your product or service. Knowledge of your product will give you the necessary answers to those objections. The most common objection will be the money. The client might say that he likes your product, but he just can't afford it at this time. Always appreciate his concern about the price and let him know that you understand. This is where you have to prove to him that he can't afford NOT to buy it at this time. Here are just a few ideas:

- The price might be changing in the near future, and it will be more expensive later, so now is the time to buy.

- If the client can't afford to pay in full, you can set him up with easy monthly payments.

- If he buys today, he will be entitled to the special discount being offered for just a short time.

- Instead of buying the large size, he could buy the smaller, less expensive size.

You may have to convince your client that something worth wanting is something worth working at getting. You might explain that people spend money each week on things they don't really need without realizing it. You may point out that your product costs no more each week than a pack of cigarettes. Help them to see that buying your product is not going to put them in the poorhouse, but instead will blend right in with their normal flow of monthly expenses and better their lives.

I won't lie to you and say that you are going to sell everyone you talk to. There are always those who, for whatever reason, will never buy. Maybe they are just too stubborn. You can't let this affect your progress. Expect it. Nobody makes a sale to each and every person he talks to. On average, I sold seven out of every ten people I presented my product to. I was told that 70 percent was a very good average. If you can sell three or four out of every ten, you will do very well. Certain products will bring a smaller average, but because of the price and commission on the product, you don't need a higher average. As far as the money objection is concerned, again I say you won't get them all, but you will get your fair share. Some people will never spend money unless it brings them self-gratification. For instance, I will never understand a person who says he can't afford $15 or $20 a month for life insurance to protect his family, but that same person will go to the casino and lose $500 as if it were nothing.

Order-Blank Close – Let's not forget what is called the order-blank close. In this close you are not giving the client a choice; instead you start filling out the order form by asking him the correct spelling of his last name or his correct mailing address. Once he gives you an answer, he has committed himself to the sale.

Puppy-dog Close – Over the years, different salespeople have used many other methods of closing for a variety of products. One of them is called the puppy-dog close. This is when you have a product that you can let the person use on a trial basis with no money or obligation. It's like giving someone a puppy to take home. After one day, they can never give him back. The object is that they will like the product so much that they will buy it because they won't want to part with it. There is a story about a small television store in Iowa. When color TVs first came out, the storeowner sold more color TV sets than any other store in the nation. He would have one on display in his store, and when a customer stopped to look at it, he would convince the customer to let him send one to his home to watch for free for two weeks. No customer could refuse that offer. After two weeks the customer had to buy it, because by now all his family, friends, and neighbors had been by to see it, and his wife and kids loved it. How could he now explain to everybody why he'd sent it back?

Ben Franklin Close – Another method of closing, used sometimes when the customer can't decide whether or not to buy, is called the Ben Franklin close. This is when the salesperson takes out a sheet of paper and draws a line down the center from top to bottom. At the top left-hand side he writes the words "good points," and on the right-hand side he writes "bad points." Then, always being sure he has a long list, he proceeds to write all the good points of his product, and all the reasons why the client should buy now. When he is finished, he turns to the client and asks him to start naming the bad points. Usually, the client can't come up with any, and don't you put any down for him. The client will see that the good points far outweigh the bad. Your next step is to give the closing question with a choice: "Do you want it in red or green?"

Tell-A-Story Close – In my business, selling life insurance, when the sale was questionable, I would tell a story. This is called the tell-a-story close. I would sit back with a somewhat sad look on my face and tell the client of how, a few years ago, I had tried to sell a man life insurance to protect his family in case something happened to him. I would confess that at the time I was a very inept salesman, and hadn't done a good job of persuading him to buy. I would explain how, several months later, I learned that the man had dropped dead of a heart attack, leaving his wife and three children to fend for themselves because he had no life insurance. The family had a hard go of it, and eventually lost their house. I would explain that, in a way, I blamed myself for their situation. This story, when told with sincerity, would put the client in the other man's shoes; he could envision his family trying to carry on without money. I would usually make the sale.

Take-It-Away Close – The take-it-away close can be used as a last resort if you can't close any other way. The psychology behind this action is the fact that when you take something away from someone, they suddenly want it. For example, a lady might get off the train each night on her way home from work, and then walk two blocks from the station to her home. Near the train station is a dress shop. Every day she stops to admire a pretty dress in the store window. As she looks at the dress each evening, she keeps telling herself that one day soon she will go in the shop to try it on and perhaps buy it. After two or three weeks, she passes the store one evening and discovers the dress is gone. Now in a panic, she runs into the store to inquire about the dress only to learn it had been sold. The lesson here is that as long as she knew she could buy the dress at any time, she didn't really want it that badly, but now that it had been taken away from her, she wanted it.

This same philosophy is used in the everyday business world. You might be driving by a new home development and see a large sign showing all the lots that are available. On several of the lots, the builder has marked in red the word "sold." In truth, the lots probably haven't been sold, but the builder wants you to think they have. He wants you to think other people are buying them up so that you might grab one before they're all gone. This same thing can be said of the night of that "last" stock sale I held, when everyone ran to the tables to buy stock before it was all gone, or how I used it on Bill and Jane, when I took the opportunity to buy a policy away from them. As soon as I took it away, they wanted it.

There were times in my career when I was in the home of a client, seated at the kitchen table, presenting my product, and no matter how hard I tried, the client wasn't buying. I would put on a sad face and begin packing up my sales materials. I would say to the client, "I'm sorry for doing such an inept job of presenting the policy, because I know that if I had been more professional, you would have seen the value of owning one." I would further apologize for not having done my job well, and tell the client not to be concerned, because I would never call on him again, and would in fact take his name off my list. As strange as this may sound, I found that people, unpredictable as they are, never wanted me to take their names off my list. For some reason, they felt they might miss out on something. You can also believe that some, though not all, of these sales were saved right then and there, because my taking it away took all the pressure off the client, who now wanted it. You never know what's going to make a person buy; that's why you need to know all you can about selling techniques.

Finally, as long as we are talking about closing, remember: When the order form is completed, and it's time for the client's signature, don't ever ask him or her to sign. The word "sign" sometimes has a bad ring to it. You are reminding the client that he is buying something. Instead, just turn the form around and ask him, "Would you okay this for me?" The word "okay" goes down a lot easier than "sign."

Timing Is Important

When you make appointments with people, whether you are going to them or they are coming to you, be on time. If you say you will be there at seven, then you should be there five minutes before, not five minutes after. If the people are coming to your office to see you, be there and be ready to see them. Don't make them wait. There is only so much time, and everyone is busy with one thing or another, so have respect for other people and for their time, because time is precious.

Other Important Tips

If, when you talk to clients about your product or service, you say you'll call back, then be darned sure you make that call, even if it's only to say you can't help them. Nothing infuriates me more than someone who says, "I'll call you back" and then doesn't. You can be sure that your client won't think highly of you, and might not want to deal with you in the future. Once, I called a Cadillac saleswoman to inquire about buying a new car. She told me she would get back to me, but she never did. That cost her a sale and probably a nice commission.

If you work for a company, regardless of the product or service it offers, and you then take a job with a different company, let your clients know that you've made a move. It's hard to build a following of clients, so why abandon yours? Chances are that many of them will follow you to your new location when they need to make their next purchase, because, if you dealt fairly and honestly with them, you're the reason they bought the product. In most cases, clients deal with the person first and the product second, and they will likely want to deal with you again when their needs warrant it. Keep your clients informed of your job changes, and you'll find that you will keep them.

How to Enter a Home

Some people might say that house calls have become a thing of the past, but I believe that with all the various products being sold in this country, there will always be a need for house calls. Whether you ever make a house call or not, the following is good to know, because you never can tell when you might find yourself in that situation. I am going to give you step-by-step instructions on how to enter a prospect's home, and put yourself at his kitchen table, which is usually the ideal place to give the presentation and make the sale. In my years with life insurance companies, I taught hundreds of men and women how to sell, and entering the home was part of the training. I believe there is a science to this procedure, and I'm not sure it's being taught anywhere today.

You start to enter the client's home as soon as you leave your home. To begin with, make sure you have a clean car. Impressions are all-important. You do not want to pull up in front of the client's home with a dirty car. It doesn't matter whether your car is new or old, but it does matter if it's clean. People know you are coming to sell them something, and, as I said earlier, they want to buy, but they might not realize it yet. A dirty car, however, takes away from the successful appearance that you need to give, and definitely will be a negative in the eyes of the client. When I say have a clean car, I mean the inside of your car should also be clean and clutter free. I have been in many cars as a passenger over the years, and when I step into someone's car and find loose tissues, loose coins, Styrofoam cups, empty fast-food bags, sneakers, and who knows what else on the floor, and I have to be careful not to step on the garbage, it just plain makes me sick. I form a lesser opinion of that person — he or she now feels unclean to me.

Your client may be able to see into your car, and if it's cluttered and dirty, he will form a lesser opinion of you. You are coming there to sell him something and take his money, and he needs to feel good about that. Seeing a cluttered car will set him to thinking you have a cluttered mind, and when it comes to his money, he wants your mind to be sharp. Appearances are crucial.

The next thing you should be is prepared. Before you arrive at the person's home, have all your sales materials ready and in the order in which you are going to use them. If you are not prepared, then get prepared before you arrive at his home. Stop your car a block or two away and get organized. If you pull up to the client's home and then sit there for five minutes fumbling around and organizing your materials, it sends the wrong message. The client and his wife might be watching you through the windows. They know you are coming there to sell them something, but if they are watching you fumble around in the car, it will be like rubbing it in their faces. They will be thinking, *look, he's preparing to sell us something*, and they are already committing themselves to not buying.

When you pull up in front of your client's home, have a clean car, have your materials ready, and open the car door and spring out with an enthusiasm about you, as if to say, "It's a great day and life is wonderful." Have a spring in your step as you go up the walkway to their front door. Always assume that the people are watching you, because they probably are, as you walk toward their house. Having a spring in your step and an enthusiastic air about you will start to put them in a buying mood. If you're excited and alive, they will feel excited and alive. If you climb out of your car slowly and looking tired, and drag yourself toward their house with a washed-out look about you, I guarantee you will not make a sale that evening. Nobody wants to give his or her hard-earned money to a washed-out-looking person.

When you get to the stairs, you climb right up them, again with a spring in your step. You ring the doorbell, and then you step back. Do not crowd them at the door when they open it. Leave room between yourself and your prospect. This will make them feel more at ease, and any fears they may have had about being high pressured will pretty much disappear. If you are carrying a case of some kind, like an attaché case or some type of briefcase or your actual product, set it down a little behind you while you wait for the doorbell to be answered. Again, you want to be high-pressure-free before them, and if you are standing there with your case in front of you so that it's the first thing they see when they open the door, you may scare them off before you even get started.

For the sake of this example, I am using a typical bungalow-type home in the city. The homes may vary depending on where you live, but the principles explained here remain the same. The door is opened and you are invited in. You take your case in one hand, and you put out your other hand and give a hearty hand-shake, like this is the best day of your life. As soon as you enter the home, lose the case. Leave it on the floor or against the wall by the door. Your client will invite you in, and you walk in leaving the case behind. You are always smiling, and you look around the room. You compliment the couple on what a fine-looking home they have and how much you like the way it is decorated, or you might make a fuss over a picture of a grandchild that's sitting out for people to see.

In the normal flow of things, the people will probably point to the sofa and ask if you would like to take a seat. Sit down while you are still marveling about the house or the décor. The couple will ask if you would like a drink or a soda or coffee. Say, 'No, thank you.' You do not want to drink coffee or soda or booze while you are there to make a sale. You can say that a nice glass of water would be wonderful. Now the Mrs. will run to the kitchen to get her guest a glass of water. At this moment, she is bonding with you. When she brings you the water, you thank her, and you drink it like it's the best water you've ever had in your life. She will be watching. Now she feels good be-cause she did something for you and you appreciated it. You liked her water.

You are sitting on the sofa, and there is a little small talk. Maybe you mention the traffic on the way there, or the good weather that everyone's been enjoying. Do not, and I mean never, talk politics or religion. You will never come out on top of a discussion in those areas. While you sit there, you size up the house and notice where the kitchen is. The small talk will come to an end. You will know when that moment comes, when everybody is looking at each other and no one knows what else to say. You only want to make small talk for a few minutes anyway. If you have very talkative people, you may have to make the move. As soon as the moment happens, you stand up, walk over to the door, pick up your case, and say, "May we go to the kitchen, please?" Then start heading toward the kitchen. Usually, the wife will jump in front of you and lead the way. This is why I told you to leave your case at the door. If you had taken it with you as you sat on the sofa, I guarantee you would have been there the entire time. Giving a presentation over a coffee table is not the ideal arrangement for making a sale. Because your case is at the door, you have a reason to get up. When you do, you take control and make the arrangement suit you.

You are now heading toward the kitchen. When you get there, politely take over. Just say to the couple, "You sit here, and you sit there, and I'll sit here, so you can more easily see what I have to show you." Don't be afraid, they will do exactly as you say — especially if you are friendly and doing it with a smile. You want to arrange the seating so that both the husband and wife are in front of you. You need to be looking at both of them at the same time. If you set it up so you are between them, or so you can see only one of them at a time, they may be giving each other signals. You must have eye contact with both people at all times. Wear a wristwatch, and at some point during your presentation take a casual glance at it, just for a second. Make sure you do it when both people are looking. Do not say anything; instead, go on with your presentation. This is a type of subliminal message:

the effect you want to achieve, and probably will achieve, is that your clients will think you're a busy man. You have someone else to see after leaving them, someone who wants to buy your product. Therefore you must be successful. You can convey all this in a split second just by looking at your watch. If they ask you if there is a problem, then confirm that you do indeed have another appointment after theirs.

When you complete your presentation and you have made the sale, put all your materials back into your case, and be sure to pick up any sheets of paper you may have scribbled on to illustrate some point or other while you were giving your presentation. You do not want to leave notes or figures that the customer can look at later, get confused about, and then want to cancel the order. When you are getting ready to leave, ask them for referrals. Ask if they know someone else who would enjoy your product as much as they will. If you ask, people will help you. You need to get referrals from everyone you can, and never be afraid to ask for them.

Knowing the technique of how to enter a home can help you even if you don't make house calls, but instead have people come to you. Some of these techniques can apply to either situation. Learn from them so they are in your mind to draw on when needed. The cleanliness, the enthusiasm, the smile, and the knowledge of your product are all parts of the impression your client will have of you, so be at your best because you never get a second chance to make a good first impression.

They Stood You Up

Every once in a while you might get stood up when you go on a call. This happens. People will stand you up, and people will hang up on you when you call them. This is part of life when you are in business. Don't let it discourage you. If things like this don't happen once in a while, then you really aren't working.

What do you do when someone stands you up? Always give that person the benefit of the doubt. There might have been an emergency, causing him not to be there. Maybe he just plain forgot. Whatever the case, when you call him the next day, don't be angry; rather, show concern that something might have happened. He will tell you. If you make a second appointment, and he stands you up again, remove him from your list and don't waste any more time on him. Some people are just plain ignorant, and they have no concern whatsoever that because of them you wasted gasoline and valuable time when you could have been seeing someone else and being productive. Instead, they caused you to lose an entire evening.

In my experience, this always seemed to happen when the client lived an hour away. I needed the business as much as anyone else, and I couldn't afford to waste my evenings, driving for an hour in one direction, only to find that the people were not at home. It's a very deflating feeling, and a long ride back home. These incidents happened when I was first starting out. For some reason, I think people can sense that fact, because when you become experienced and good at what you do, it doesn't seem to happen anymore. I had to find a way to assure that the people were home before I made such a long trip. I certainly didn't want to call them before I left, because that would just give them an opportunity to cancel the appointment. I came up with a brainstorm.

Say I had an appointment set for 7:00 p.m. I would have my wife call the client about 5:30 or so. If they answered the phone, we knew they were home. Now, in order to assure that they would still be there when I arrived, my wife would tell them that I had been out on calls all day, and my book showed that I was scheduled to be at their house at 7:00. She would sound a little panicky, and tell them it was an emergency and that she had no way of getting hold of me. She would ask if they could please have me call home as soon as I got there. The people would, of course, say yes. Now I would leave the house and make the long drive to them. When I would arrive, the people were not only waiting for me, but more often than not they would be waiting by the front door, waving at me to hurry in. They would take me right to their phone, and tell me to call home to deal with an emergency. I would act surprised and concerned, and I would call home. Can you imagine? Within seconds I was in a complete stranger's house and using their phone. Now that's power! After a few minutes of playacting with the wife, I would say, loud enough for all to hear, "I will hurry up and take care of these people, then I'm on my way." When I finished the call, I would tell the people I had a sick child and had to get a prescription on the way home before the drugstore closed at 9:00. They knew I had a long way to go home, so they would always let me skip the preliminaries and get right to the subject at hand, the insurance. They always bought, usually right away, because I had become human to them and gained their trust. I didn't use this scenario often, but when I did, it always worked. Keep in mind that there were no cell phones or pagers back then. If there had been we could have said I'd forgotten my cell phone at home.

I definitely do not want to give you the impression that it's okay to be dishonest. It is not, because being honest is always the right thing to do. It shows your character, and your success, when you reach it, will be solid. That said, every once in a while you have to do what you have to do. I was never dishonest to these people about my product. I just exaggerated about my personal circumstances.

One More Exaggeration

Again, sometimes you have to do what you have to do. A friend of mine thought I should include this story because he liked it so much. When a person starts an insurance agency from scratch, as I did in 1976, it doesn't mean insurance companies are going to come knocking on your door to represent them. The fact is they don't want you, because you have no track record and you can't guarantee them a certain amount of business. Most companies want you to already be representing three companies and show three years of experience with them. If nobody wants to be the first one, then it's very hard to get three.

What happens is you have to place your business through other established agents and share the commissions. You can then work at building up enough volume that you can finally get a company to stick their neck out and give you a chance. This, of course, was what I had to do. After some time, I finally got a couple of companies to roll the dice and give me a contract.

There was a third company, which I really wanted very badly. I spoke to the field representative and sold him on giving me a contract. He wanted to give me one, but explained that it wasn't up to him to make the final decision. He said he had to bring out a company officer to approve me, and warned me that my chances were not very good. He told me that the company officer would be very tough, and would grill me excessively as to what I could do for the company.

My agency consisted of a secretary and myself, and business was scarce. We were alerted as to when they were coming for the interview, and we were prepared. My secretary had prearranged for numerous of her friends and family to start calling our office at a designated time and then continue to call.

I have always loved good artwork, and on the wall behind my desk was a Western print of a man on horseback riding in the rain, which was part of my collection. The artist's last name was Harvey. When the two gentlemen arrived at my office, the field rep introduced me to the company officer. We shook hands and then sat down. He looked at the print on the wall behind me and asked, "Is that a Harvey?" I almost fell off my chair with surprise and answered yes. He then asked if I had any other prints and who the artists were. I told him of my collection and various artists. It turns out he was a collector also, and liked many of the prints I owned.

Meanwhile, the phones were ringing off the hook, giving the impression we were busy. After talking art for about thirty minutes, the company officer turned to the field man, who by now was dumbfounded, and said, "Go ahead and give him a contract. He'll be all right." The field man sat there with a dropped jaw, and nodded "Okay." During the entire visit, the subject of insurance or what I could do for the company had never come up once. I guess I got the contract due to one half "sting" and the other half art. You never know what's going to make a person tick. It was a very good day.

Ask and You Shall Receive

I touched earlier on the fact that you must ask for referrals. After you have made your list of prospects and are working that list, keep asking people you know for referrals so your list continues to grow. The best source for referrals is the person who just bought your product or service. If they just bought, they must certainly like it and are happy with it; otherwise they would not have done business with you. If you conducted yourself in the style I have explained, and formed the habits of enthusiasm, friendliness, and smiling all the time, your client will like you. When clients like you, they are more than happy to help you. All you need to do is ask.

For some reason, many salespeople are afraid to ask. Maybe they're afraid the client might get angry with them. This is far from the truth. People really like to help others. It makes them feel good, so if you're not afraid to ask, people will give you referrals, hopefully, more than you can handle.

In my definition of asking, I also mean doing your own prospecting. When I'm prospecting for customers to buy my insurance, I call it asking. When I am saying to the person that I might be able to save him some money, I'm asking. If I'm not asking, I'm not going to sell any insurance. I also bring up the subject of life insurance to all of my clients. It's amazing how many don't have any, but because I ask, I write a record number of life policies each year.

I stated earlier that you wouldn't go up to someone and ask, "Hey, do you want to buy my product?" However, there are some exceptions to the rule. When you are experienced at what you are doing, there may be a time when you can be so bold. This would be when you have discussed your product with a client previously, you know he is interested, but for some reason just can't get himself to make the decision. He probably never will make the decision until someone gives him a nudge. That someone would be you. Many times, when I have previously spoken to someone about insurance and I know that they want it, I would just say upon seeing them, "Why don't we sit down now and take care of the insurance we talked about? This is a good time for me, and besides, you really need it." After that, I would simply take out the paperwork and ask him the correct spelling of his name. Remember the order-blank close?

Sometimes, when you ask for something, you might be

surprised by what you receive. A number of years ago, a woman looking for homeowners insurance called me. The company I was selling for at the time required a photo of the home with the application. I learned a long time ago that as an insurance man I didn't have to run here and there going on calls or taking photos. It was just as easy to ask the customer to send a photo with his or her check, or if it was a customer who needed to buy insurance but wanted to see me, rather than say, "I will come out," I found it just as easy to ask, "When would it be convenient for you to stop by?" I have never had anyone say no and refuse to come to my office. The fact that they drive to my office is usually a guarantee they are going to buy. I save a lot of time by using this technique, and I save gasoline, which as you know is expensive.

Getting back to the woman who needed a homeowner's policy, I took her information over the phone, and asked her to send me a photo and a check. Because I asked, I did receive. A couple of days later, an envelope arrived at my office. I happily opened it, because I knew it meant a new piece of business, and I pulled out her check. Next, I pulled out the photo so I could see what the house looked like, and to my surprise she had sent me a portrait photo of herself with a big smile. If you ask for something, you will receive it.

Summary

In this chapter, I have given you a concise outline of the basic principles of selling, as I know them. There are scores of books out there that say pretty much what I have just told you, and some give more precise details of certain aspects. What I have described worked for me, and still works to this day. If you can master the principles in this book, you will do just fine. In fact, you should do very well. I am not discouraging you from seeking more knowledge and honing your skills and reading other books, but an abundance of knowledge is useless unless you get out and start selling. Until you do that, knowledge may only serve to clog your brain. Some people are what we call professional students, who go to school to learn everything. They are usually very smart, but the one thing they don't learn in school is how to make money, and many of these educated people can't hold a job because they're just too smart for it. So I say to you, keep it simple. You have enough here to get your feet wet and to find out just what you can do. If you don't succeed, more knowledge may not necessarily help much. If you do succeed, then learn all you can, but don't overdue it to the point where you forget how to be practical. People like dealing with regular people, and don't you forget that.

Chapter ten

Going Into Business
Opening Your Own Shop

You are now ready to go into business. You have learned your product, you know your service, you have set your goals, you are motivated and thinking positively, and in your mind it's time to go. Let me warn you of two things that could happen when you go into business for yourself. The first is that when you go out on your own, you will discover a newfound freedom. All of a sudden you will be your own boss. You can schedule your day as you see fit. You can go to lunch when you want to, take as much time as you need, and even take time to run errands for yourself if you so desire. However, if you're sincere about making it on your own, you will be working more hours than you've ever worked in your life — but it won't seem like work, because you are working for yourself. When you are self-employed, you have no boss telling you what to do or when to do it. The thing I want to warn you about is that once you get the taste of being on your own, you can never go back to working for someone else. That would be the hardest thing you could ever have to do. You will be spoiled by being on your own, and no matter what, you will have to make it.

The second thing I want to warn you about is that once you go into business for yourself, everybody will think you are rich. To your family, your friends and your relatives, you become the rich guy or the rich gal. Even though you are not, and you will have to work very hard to get there, they will still think it. This is something you will just have to learn to live with.

So far, I have preached about you knowing what you want and going for it. I am not trying to throw a negative into the mix at this time, but I want you to still think practically while you are going for it. Everybody is coming from a different living situation at the time that he or she decides to go into business. You may be a single person, still living at home with Mom and Dad, or you might be a married man or woman with two or three children, and you are the main, or even the only, breadwinner in your household. You want to be absolutely sure that you are ready to take the plunge and are prepared for some possible lean times until you get your business off the ground.

When I first entered the business world with the Decatur Company, I knew what I wanted and was sure I could do it. However, I had a wife and two children, and I did not want to jeopardize them in any way, or disrupt their well-being and the way of life we were accustomed to. Although I was successfully selling life insurance, I knew it would still take time for the money to catch up and start coming in on a steady basis, so for that reason I did not quit my regular job.

I have known managers and company executives whose philosophy was to find the guy who was in debt up to his ears, with a family, a mortgage, car payments, and whatnot, because he would work harder and produce more than most other people. If the guy weren't in debt, they would encourage him to get into debt by suggesting that he buy a new car or a new home.

I am not going to argue with the philosophy of those people, because for the most part it works. I am going to say, however, that I myself worked part-time for one whole year before I took the plunge and quit my regular job. I didn't want or need the stress of possibly hurting my family and myself financially. I had to be comfortable in going full-time and have peace of mind at the same time.

If you are a single person, still living at home, you may not have all of these concerns, and might be in a better position to change careers and not look back. If you are married, have a family, and are the main breadwinner, be sure you're ready before you go ahead. There is no disgrace in working your craft part-time for a while until you get your feet on the ground.

I would encourage everyone: learn your craft, work hard, and build for the future. I would not encourage anyone to up and quit his job to try something new to see if he can be successful at it. Learn, work, build, and when you are ready you will know it. You are going to face enough hurdles when you go into business for yourself, and you don't need the stress of not knowing how you are going to buy groceries for your family. When I managed my territory with the Decatur Company, and when I managed the Oak Lawn Company, we hired people part-time, and never did I tell anyone to quit his job till he knew he was ready.

Having said this, I don't mean that you should procrastinate and put off making the big decision forever, because if you do, you will never reach and fully experience the heights you were intended to reach. There is something to be said for burning your bridges behind you and never looking back. When you do, there is only one way to move, and that is forward. When one really has to accomplish something, and has nowhere else to go, that person will usually accomplish what he or she set out to do.

The only person to blame if you don't make it is yourself. The incentive to make it will be far greater if you burn your bridges than if you had a crutch to lean on, and nobody wants to blame himself or herself for his own failure.

Working Out of Your Home

Working out of your home, or running a business out of your home, is something a lot of people do, especially at the beginning of their careers, but there are both positives and negatives to working out of your home. One of the positives is you won't have anywhere near the operating expenses you would have if you had a store or office. One of the negatives is that if you aren't a self-starter, it will become pretty hard to build your business. People who work out of their homes need stamina and drive to move ahead, grow, and become successful.

When I went into the life insurance business full-time, I worked out of my house. I had a small room in the basement of my home that I called my office. At first I got up and left the house and hustled every day, prospecting for clients, and cold calling. But as time went on, I found myself sleeping later, watching the morning TV shows, doing household chores, and wasting most of my workday. None of this was making me money. I realized soon enough that an office in the home was not for me. It was making me lazy. I'm the type of person who needs a place to go each morning. Once I recognized that, I made arrangements to rent desk space from a friend of mine who owned an insurance agency. Once I had rented the space, I had a place to go. I told myself I had to start my day from my desk at a certain time each morning, and I kept to that decision. I made sure I was there every morning, and from there I went about my day. I became more productive and began growing again. It was just too hard for me to work out of my home, because there were too many distractions.

For some people, working out of the home is fine. It works, and it works well. It's all in the makeup of the person. Some businesses are more adaptable to the home than others are. For instance, you wouldn't run an auto-body repair business from your home, but a hairdresser working out of her home, with her sink and chair in her basement salon, might do very well. You may also hear that there are tax advantages to working out of your home, but don't be fooled: There are some advantages, but the IRS has specific rules as to what you can and can't deduct. Before you start taking deductions, sit down with a qualified, trusted tax person or CPA.

Partnerships

Some people think it's a good idea to go into business together, and decide to form a partnership involving two or more people. Depending on what type of business you are forming, a partnership can be an ideal situation, because there is more than one person out there building the company and working together toward the same goal. Partnerships can be good and very successful; however, partnerships can also be very destructive and fail miserably. I have seen far more partnerships fail than succeed. Why should this be?

In my years of running an insurance agency, I have met many people, both men and women, who came to me announcing that they are going into business together and want business insurance. They come in all excited, patting each other on the back, and eager to go. I would look at these people, and something in my gut would tell me it was not going to work. Almost like clockwork, within ninety days one of them would be back in my office, telling me what a rotten SOB the other one was, even though they may have been the best of friends all their lives. I've seen this happen too many times to come up with a total.

The most common underlying reason is because when people go into business as partners, they fail to draw up plans for the responsibilities of all the parties. If you are planning a partnership, sit all the partners down at a table, and list all the necessary duties your company expects each of you to perform. After you have made the list, divide the duties among the partners so that everyone knows who is responsible for doing what. If everyone knows what his responsibility is, there will be far less chance of arguments, and a greater chance for success.

Best friends or not, money changes people. When there is no definite plan for responsibilities, each partner will feel that he is working harder, devoting more time to the business, carrying the others, and deserves a greater share of the profits. After watching partnership after partnership dissolve I began coaching newcomers in the pros and cons of partnership and what they should look out for. I would encourage them to draw up a responsibility agreement spelling out each party's duties. Some listened, but most did not, because they all thought such problems would never affect such good friends as they were.

I offer you this advice whether you are entering into a partnership agreement or a corporate arrangement. (Note: Being a corporation does offer some tax advantages — talk to your CPA. As far as duties are concerned, corporate officers are no different from partners. Corporations also fail.) As for me, because of the experiences I lived through, I will never build and operate a business again unless I own or control it. Remember, I didn't want a contract because I thought all the men in the Oak Lawn Company were my friends. Money changes people.

Beware of the Gold Digger

Let's remember the old Mother Goose story about the hen that wanted to bake bread for her chicks. Because she knew it was going to be a big job, she went to all the other barnyard animals and asked for their help. She asked the pig, the cow, the horse, the rabbit, and all the rest. Everyone could see how much work it was going to be, so they all made excuses as to why they couldn't help her. Determined to bake the bread, the hen realized she would have to do it alone. Knowing how much work was required, she started early in the morning and worked hard all day. Finally, at the end of the day she was finished and had several loaves of fresh-baked bread. The good aroma of the bread spread throughout the barnyard. Before long, all the barnyard animals came to the hen and offered to help her eat the bread. The hen told them that since they hadn't helped her bake it, they could not eat any of it.

The hen did all the work, and all the others wanted to share in the fruits of her labor. After you have started your business and you are doing well, people may come along and want to be part of it. They will bend over backward to help you, offering to take some of the workload off your shoulders and relieve you of some of the stress. They will praise you, stroke your ego, and make you feel like you are the greatest person they ever met. Beware of their true motive.

You have started a successful business, and to the person on the outside looking in, it looks darn good. They want a piece of the business you worked so hard to build. They may say that they want to be your partners. Be very careful. After you did all the work, there is no reason in the world why you should give up half your business to someone else. If you really think you need that person, then hire him as an employee. It is your business, and you should always have and keep control. Over the years, I have had more than one person try to weasel their way into owning part of the agency I built with my hard work and sacrifice.

Renting Space

If you will not be working out of your home, you'll probably be renting space somewhere. Whether it's office space, warehouse space, or a storefront, expenses come with it, and you must be prepared for them. There are expenses that are common to all businesses, and there are some expenses that apply only to specific businesses. The following is a list of general expenses that apply to almost all businesses:

- Rent;
- Electricity;
- Gas;
- Phone;
- Postage;
- Water;
- Insurance;
- Toiletries (toilet paper, paper towels, soap, etc.);
- Janitorial or cleaning service (unless the owner or the employees do it).

Depending on what kind of business you are operating, certain of those general expenses may cost you more than they would cost other businesses. For instance, if you are operating a beauty salon, your water bill will be much higher than, let's say, an office.

Some businesses use more postage than others, especially if they do a lot of mailings. Any type of sales operation will run up your phone bill. It is safe to say, however, that if you use the phone in sales, your phone bill will be directly proportional to your income. Usually, the higher the phone bill the higher your income.

A variety of other expenses will be unique to certain types of businesses. Depending on what type of business you are in, you may have to purchase some of the following:

◆ Office furniture;

◆ Store fixtures;

◆ Office equipment and supplies;

◆ Computers;

◆ Tools or supplies;

◆ Merchandise;

◆ Copy machine;

◆ Fax machine;

◆ Postage machine;

◆ Internet access;

◆ Alarm system;

◆ City or state license fees;

◆ Self-employment tax.

When you work as someone's employee, they must match your Social Security withholding tax. When you are self-employed, you must match it, which means you pay both halves. *Tax laws, of course, are subject to change.*

If You Have Employees

When you have employees, you must, of course, withhold Social Security tax from their paychecks, but as the employer, you must match the amount withheld.

Unemployment Tax is a tax that all employers pay. This tax goes into the unemployment system from which people who are out of work draw unemployment.

Some people confuse workers' compensation insurance with unemployment tax, but they are not the same. Workers' compensation is insurance; unemployment tax is a tax.

The preceding list of expenses, even though no one type of business would require all of them, might be enough to scare the pants off of anyone planning to go into business. It is not my intention to scare or discourage you. However, this may help you understand more clearly why I stressed the point about being ready before you take that big step. If you can, stay part-time until there is a steady cash flow coming in from your business, and work from home if you can, until such time as your business demands you move on in order for it to have greater growth.

Insurance

If you are going into business you will need insurance. Do not underestimate the importance of having insurance and having the right kind of insurance. People have been sued and have lost their homes because they were not properly insured. Different businesses call for different types of insurance; there is no "one size fits all." Sit down with a trusted insurance professional and ask advice on what type of insurance you will need for your particular business. Also, now that you are self-employed, keep in mind that you will have to provide your own health and life insurance, and your own retirement program such as an IRA or 401k plan.

Good News: Tax Deductions

Now that I've scared you with expenses, I have some good news: Being in business for yourself opens up a whole arena of tax deductions, which you don't have when you are someone's employee. True, an employee doesn't have the expenses either, but let's weigh the options. As a self-employed person, if you use your car for business, your gasoline is deductible, toll fees and parking fees are deductible if they are business related, and your car's cost and maintenance would also be fully or partially deductible.

Any type of supplies you buy for your business — pencils, pens, paper, computers, and virtually anything you need to run the business — is deductible. If you take a client to lunch or dinner, a portion of the bill can be deducted. Your phone, lights, heat, rent, license fees, and interest on business charge cards or business loans are all deductible. Except for life insurance premiums, all other insurance premiums, including health insurance, are deductible. There are a number of other areas that can also be deductible. So yes, as a self-employed individual you will incur expenses, but most if not all of them are tax deductible, which pretty much evens the field. To know exactly how deductions will affect your particular business, let a qualified accountant or CPA advise you.

Payroll Services

Some small businesses find it advantageous to use a payroll service to cut checks for employees, keep track of the taxes withheld, and do much of the paperwork and record keeping. This can take a huge burden off the shoulders of the owner, and may even be cheaper than using an accountant or CPA.

A Tax Tip You Should Know

There is a tax fact that many people may not know. Rental income is not subject to self-employment tax. Only wages from your corporation, or your net profits if you are not a corporation, are subject to the tax. This means that if you are fortunate enough to own rental properties, you will not be paying self-employment tax on the rental income. However, being a landlord entails other expenses and headaches, which may nullify whatever savings you may have.

Let's say you reach the point where you are in a position to buy your own building or office condo for your business. If your business is a corporation, this information might save you quite a bit of money. Let's say that your business pays you a salary of $6,000 per month. Now you purchase a building or condo office. Instead of your business buying the property and then paying the mortgage on it, buy the property under your personal name and put it in trust. Now let your business pay you rent. Let's say the rent it pays you is $3,000 per month. You can now lower the salary side of your income to $3,000 per month instead of $6,000, and therefore only pay self-employment tax on $3,000 instead of $6,000. For a self-employed person, that means an approximate 15% savings on the $3,000 of rental income, which comes out to about $450 per month. You still have to pay the mortgage, but you would have to pay it anyway, whether personally or from the business. In the end, depending on the amounts of the salary and the rent, this could translate into thousands of dollars of savings each year.

Keep One Eye on Expenses

My purpose in breaking down the business expenses is to open your mind to what you may expect when you go into business for yourself. Too many people think going into business is easy, especially when opening up a store or shop. Their eyes are blinded by visions of profit, without ever thinking they may have expenses that offset those profits. They never think of or plan for all the hidden expenses that come with going into business. Too few plan for those expenses; in fact they don't plan ahead at all. Poor planning can put you in financial stress while you are just leaving the starting gate.

Before you take the step into your own business, look at your current everyday household expenses. Review them, and see where you may be able to cut them down. Every household has some waste of money that could be curtailed. Look at your cable bill, your phone bill, your gas and electric, and even your grocery bill. Talk to your cable and utilities companies and tell them you need to cut back. They may point out features you are paying for that you really don't need, and help you find ways to lower your bill. Even your grocery bill can be lowered if you don't buy some of the unnecessary items and junk foods that you don't need anyway. If you look, you may also find other areas in your weekly expenses that can be cut down or eliminated altogether. I bring all this to your attention because when you first go into business you have to keep one eye not only on your business expenses but your home expenses as well, because you want to have every edge you can possibly have.

Whether or not you go into your own business, and whether or not you try to improve on your employment situation, the following two pieces of advice can still be of great help to you. In fact, if this is all that you gain from reading this book, it will have all been worth it. First, control your credit card debt, and if you can, get rid of it altogether. This is one area that can really take a bite out of your financial situation. Interest and charges on credit cards are ridiculously high and can definitely affect your household cash flow. If you use credit cards as a convenience, pay them off each month as you get the bills. If you have large balances on your credit cards, try to curtail further use until you get those balances down and reduce your debt. Pay more each month than the required minimum payment; if all you pay is the minimum, you will never be out of credit card debt, and you will be paying over and over again for the items you purchased with those cards.

Secondly, if you have a mortgage on your home, ask your bank for an amortization schedule, even if you have to pay for it. An amortization schedule is the listing of all your monthly payments over the life of your mortgage. It breaks down how much of your payment goes to interest and how much to principal. You may be shocked. At the beginning of a mortgage you may have a $1200 monthly payment and find that only $60 is being applied to principal. This means that if you send an additional $60, you will have shortened your payments by one at the end of the term. If you are starting out with a thirty-year mortgage, it is highly possible that for a few hundred extra dollars of payment in the first year, you can knock ten years off your mortgage. If you continue to pay extra money each month toward principal you will save thousands of dollars of interest payments and have a mortgage-free home in less than ten years. If for some reason you can't obtain an amortization schedule, pay as much additional principal each month as you can to reduce the amount you owe. Regardless of how many years into your mortgage you currently are, start paying extra principal each month. You will never regret that you paid your home off earlier than the life of the mortgage.

When opening up your own store, shop, or office, the best advice I can give to you is to have a "cushion" — a certain amount of money set aside to be used only for the needs of the business. This helps to prevent you from falling behind while you're trying to get on your feet. I would recommend your cushion be equal to six months' worth of expenses. If you don't have a cushion, you may arrange a loan or a line of credit that you can draw on, with your bank. As you start to grow, take some of the profits and set them aside in a slush or emergency fund for the business. Even if we are talking only pennies in the beginning, keep adding to this fund no matter what. This is money that you will need for a rainy day. All businesses have good streaks, but they will also have slow streaks, especially during an economic downturn. If you always have an emergency fund that can carry you from six months to a year, you should be able to weather all storms.

When I first entered the business world, a friend of mine said to me, "Always keep one eye on expenses." He was so right. Many a business has failed because the person in charge wasn't paying enough attention and the expenses got him. I'm not talking only about big expenses, but also the little ones that can nickel and dime you out of business. If you are starting a business from scratch, you'd better figure that it is going to take a good three years before that business is holding its own and you can start to see the money trickling out. It could take longer, but three years is a fair estimate. If you can get past the beginning hurdles, your work and sacrifice should pay off tenfold, because as your business continues to grow you will reap rewards far greater than if you worked for someone.

When you first open up, you don't need the latest state-of-the-art equipment. You don't need the finest in furniture or the newest, most expensive phone system and computers. Buy furniture that looks nice but is not so expensive. Get a phone system and computers that fit your needs. You can get the more expensive ones later. Many people think that if they don't have the latest in everything, their business will suffer. If you don't have to spend a lot of money, don't. You do not need to go overboard. People are going to be dealing with you, not with the price of your phone system; how much you paid for this or that isn't going to make a difference as long as you are taking care of their needs.

When I first opened my insurance agency in 1976, the only money I had to my name was the $7,000 mentioned earlier. I bought used office furniture for about $200, which served me well for several years, and I brought my old portable college typewriter from home. In 1976, there were no fax machines, only the rich businesses could afford a copier, and computers were still in their infancy. No small businesses had them. For our customer records, we used three-by-five index cards, and kept them in a file box. For copies, we used carbon paper. We had a simple office, but the work got done and the business grew, and I made money. I didn't have to spend a lot on anything. Today, people close shop because the fax machine or the computer is down.

Don't Forget to Hustle

Now that you are in business, remember: the work starts now, and you probably have to work harder than ever in the beginning to make sure you get over the humps and succeed. I have known more than a few people who got as far as having their business cards printed, and then they sat back expecting the phone to ring. It doesn't work that way. You have to get out and let everyone know what you do and where you are located. I said this in a previous chapter, but I will say it again: You have to **See the people, see the people, see the people.**

Chapter eleven

A Live Audience

Speaking before audiences is certainly not something that everyone reading this book will be doing. For most people it isn't even something they will seek to do. Even if you think you will never speak before a group of people, you can never really say for sure. You may become so successful in your business that you might be asked to speak at a Rotary Club or Lions Club or chamber of commerce meeting, or appear at a high school or college to talk to students. Whatever the case, you are sure to pick up some important pointers here.

Others reading this book might do a lot of public speaking in their careers. You might become a company manager or vice president, which means you would be holding meetings with the people working for you. You may have to lead and motivate your people, or set guidelines for them. To be effective, you should have some basic knowledge of how to hold a meeting and how to speak.

Still others might find themselves giving presentations to groups of people for the purpose of selling a product, like I did so many times with the life insurance companies. Finally, some reading this book might end up doing public speaking or motivational speaking as a profession. I don't claim to be an expert, but I have spoken at close to 2,000 meetings or gatherings in my career. Audience size varied, averaging forty or fifty; the largest was at a banquet for 1,200 people. So I am sure that sharing with you the knowledge I gained by experience will help you to be a better speaker.

The art of being a good speaker and holding a successful meeting starts with your actual ability to speak — your voice. There are numerous other subtleties that can make a meeting a good one or a bad one. I will outline several areas that can affect a meeting. If the speaker could control all of these areas, I have no doubt the meeting would be a very good one. Unfortunately, the speaker doesn't always have control over all aspects of a meeting. Often the speaker does not have control because someone else is setting up the arrangements. Most meetings are held in restaurants that have meeting rooms, or in banquet-hall meeting rooms.

Room Arrangement

In my experience, the average number of people at most meetings is between thirty-five and forty. We will talk about larger audiences a little later. For an average meeting, if you have the opportunity to control the room arrangement, then by all means exercise your control.

The ideal table arrangement would be square or long rectangular tables, arranged U-style. Round tables are the least desirable. The opening of the U is where the speaker stands to speak. The tables should be arranged so that the door to the room is behind the closed side of the U. That way, if someone has to leave the room for any reason, that person won't be walking past the speaker or in front of the speaker to get out. When that happens, there is a disruption in the speaker's momentum, and though it may be a small one, it's still a disruption. The audience will temporarily lose their concentration because they are watching the person who is walking out. A few minutes later that same person will walk back into the room and cause another disruption.

Restaurant workers may also be coming and going through that same door. They are usually not as quiet as an audience member. In fact, I've been in situations where the restaurant workers talked loudly to each other, without a care for whom they might be disturbing. This too will cause subtle disruptions, because audience members will always look to see what's going on.

Noise

When booking a meeting room, the person doing the booking should determine whether the room is soundproof or at least semi-soundproof. Check with the restaurant manager to see what activities are going on in the adjacent rooms at the time of your meeting. I have been at meetings when there were similar meetings in adjacent rooms that were not a bit soundproof. This meant that each speaker had to talk louder to be heard above the other speaker. To the audience, this is very distracting and not conducive to productivity or sales. I once had the misfortune of speaking at a Saturday evening meeting that someone else booked for me. In the banquet room next to us was a wedding reception with a live band. We had over sixty people at our meeting, and like it or not, the show had to go on. I had to shout at the top of my lungs throughout the entire presentation. I wouldn't wish that situation on anyone. Afterward, I set a new rule: no Saturday night meetings under any circumstances. I also made sure we never booked at that restaurant again, because the restaurateur knew what kind of meetings we held, knew that we needed a quiet atmosphere, and should have told us there was a wedding booked at the same time.

Another area often overlooked is the overhead music that most restaurants and banquet halls have piped into the rooms. Remember to ask the manager to cut off the music before you start your meeting. When you are eating, you hardly notice the music, but when it's quiet and it's time to speak, you suddenly hear it loud and clear.

Lighting

The room in which you will be speaking must be properly lit. You want the audience to see you and just as important, you want to see them. You need to read their faces while you are speaking or giving your presentation. You need to feel their reaction because it will help you know if you need to adjust your speaking voice, or if you need to stress different points in your speech. You also need proper lighting so the audience can see your chalkboard or presentation material that you may be using.

If the room is too dark, people may tend to get drowsy and nod off while you are speaking. A well-lighted room will keep your audience awake and alive, and will also help keep their eyes on you at all times.

If you are holding a dinner meeting, the lights are sometimes dimmed a bit while people are eating. For some reason people think they need the atmosphere. No matter the level of the lights during dinner, be sure they are up before the speaker begins. Know where the light switches are before the meeting begins, so that your people aren't holding up the show while they run around looking for them. When you appear unorganized, it sends a subliminal message to your audience: they may think your company is unorganized, and no one wants to do business with a company they feel is unorganized.

Food and Drink

Meetings may vary from full-dinner meetings to coffee-only meetings or meetings with no food or drink at all. If your meeting is a breakfast, lunch, or dinner meeting, the food part should come before the speaking begins. Let everyone eat, and make sure the busboys and servers are finished coming and going. You do not want to be speaking with servers still moving among the audience, and busboys clanging dishes or silverware. Also, after people have eaten, they feel better, are more comfortable, and will be in a more receptive mood to buy, if it's a sales-type meeting.

If it's a coffee-only meeting, the coffee urns are usually left on the table for the guests to help themselves, so you probably would not have the problem of servers coming and going. It is a good idea for the person in charge to tell the servers or the manager not to interrupt once the meeting gets started.

At any meeting, a beverage is always a good idea. Coffee, soda, and juice are all acceptable. You do not — I repeat — YOU DO NOT ever want booze or alcohol at a meeting. Alcohol of any type only serves to disrupt the concentration of the attendees, because the booze can affect their thinking or reasoning. In addition, I believe serving booze at any meeting is unprofessional. When alcohol is served, you also encounter the problem of the servers coming and going, taking drink orders, not to mention the extra time all this takes. When the meeting is over, if one wants to, that is the time buy drinks for the guests, and that would be perfectly all right.

I have witnessed many meetings where alcohol was served — but never one of mine. I have seen meetings become complete disasters due to alcohol being served. When people start drinking before they eat, they tend to get drunk. I have seen men pass out with their face in a plate of food. I have seen people get into arguments over stupid things because they couldn't hold their liquor. I have seen people leave meetings drunk or tipsy and drive themselves home in snowy and icy weather, endangering themselves and the lives of others. If someone had an accident and was injured, both the restaurant and your company could be liable. If you want your meeting not to be the best that it can be, then go ahead and serve alcohol.

A tip you should remember is to tell the restaurant manager you want no alcohol served during your meeting, including the dinner part. Also instruct the restaurant that if a guest requests a drink, even if he offers to pay for it himself, the server should politely say, "I'm not permitted to serve alcohol now, but drinks will be available after the meeting." Most people will understand. If someone gets angry about it, you probably don't want to do business with that person anyway.

Introducing the Speaker

Your presentation should not last more than forty-five minutes. Any longer and you will lose the attention of the guests. If the meeting you are holding is of a formal type, by which I mean a dinner and sales presentation, then it is fitting for the speaker to be announced. One of the company members, likely the one who arranged or is in charge of the meeting, should make the introduction.

Before beginning the introduction, he should announce that the meeting will start in fifteen minutes, and that anyone who needs to use the restrooms should please take this time to do it. After the break, he resumes his position in front of the group, thanks everyone for coming, and says that he hopes they enjoyed their dinner. He takes this time to ask everyone in a very friendly way to please turn their chairs around so they can face the front. This is especially important when the tables are round and half the audience is seated with their backs to you. He might make a joke about this, something like "I don't want anyone to get a stiff neck from stretching to see." He also asks everyone to please shut off all cell phones.

Now it's time to introduce the speaker. Keep the introduction short and to the point. Mention one or two of the speaker's accomplishments; with excitement in his voice, say he is dynamic, and then announce him. Usually everyone will applaud.

Side Note

I would now like to share with you a little technique I used when I was the speaker at hundreds of dinner meetings. I would never enter the room until dinner was being served. My place was at the end of the table, just a few steps from where I would speak, and my spot was always reserved. I would stay completely out of sight. The reason for this was that the attendees knew they were going to get a sales pitch of some kind about something very good. They would wonder who was the guy that was going to present it. My not being seen until everyone was being served added a little mystery to the mix. Also, by not being available before dinner, I avoided people coming up to me to ask what the product was and how it worked. I wanted no questions — all questions would be answered during my presentation. If a guest asked one of our company members the same questions before the presentation started, he would just answer that the speaker would explain all.

When I finally did take my place at the table, no one could get to me to ask questions because dinner was being served, but I would have most of their eyes on me the whole time, wondering "Who is this guy?" In addition, I was always dressed sharp and professional looking, because when you speak, you always want to look successful, never tired and worn-out. The mystery about me kept their attention, and, I believe, had a helpful effect on sales.

As far as the dinner was concerned, I never overindulged. I would eat, but not enough to feel full. It's hard to give a good presentation and look and act excited when you're stuffed. I always made sure to eat a little dessert, which was always vanilla ice cream, because that was what we prearranged. I found that a couple of spoons of ice cream would settle the stomach. It's no fun when you are speaking to an audience and your stomach starts to bother you.

Stage Fright

It's okay to feel a little nervous before speaking to an audience. This is all very normal. There is always a tendency to be a little scared before going on. Even professional entertainers experience butterflies before performing. But once you get up there and start speaking, it all goes away. In just a few minutes you will feel comfortable and right at home. Remember: you are the professional, and you know more about your subject than your audience does.

He's the Speaker

There are many marks of a good speaker. To begin with, you had better know your product, backward, forward, upside down, and side ways. Be as knowledgeable as you can. It will reflect in your talk. I never used a microphone, as my voice could be heard at the back of the room. If you do need to use a microphone, hold it in your hand. Do not stand behind a podium.

I would thank everyone for coming, and I always assured the audience that no one was going to try to sell them anything. I always made a joke: "We have all of your license-plate numbers anyway." This would bring some laughter and relieve the tension.

I always started with a joke — a clean joke — and I always had several funny ones to choose from. Everyone would laugh. Once you get the people to laugh, they feel better, they are happy they are there, and they like you. Once they like you, the sale is easier to make.

I would then begin the presentation. I used a chalkboard to illustrate our product and how it worked. While speaking, I would be animated. I would walk around and sometimes walk right up into the U. I would make eye contact with the people as I walked up and down. This made everything more professional and down-to-earth. When you speak, move around. Make the people's eyes follow you here and there. It keeps them interested, awake, and alert.

Every once in a while I would clap my hands, just a single clap, when I was stressing a point. Again, a well-placed clap keeps the audience's attention on you at all times.

Inject some humor, if you can, at specific points during the presentation. I would make a short humorous comment here and there as I gave the presentation. Again, it keeps the audience attentive and interested, and makes you more human.

Talk loudly enough for everyone to hear. Don't shout, but project your voice and raise it or lower it at the right times to stress a certain point you want your audience to hear and digest. I have been at meetings where the speakers talked so softly that only the people up front could hear. The rest of the room could not, and therefore lost interest; their minds wandered, and some even went to sleep. Nobody ever fell asleep at my meetings.

Again, as a speaker you should be animated. Do not stand in one spot, never moving, or your voice will automatically become a monotone and your audience will lose interest. A good entertainer moves around onstage, always keeping the audience alive.

Live and Appearing Onstage

I remember the 1992 presidential election very well. My wife and I were in our living room, watching the first debates on TV. The candidates running were the incumbent, President George H. Bush, billionaire H. Ross Perot, and the somewhat unknown Bill Clinton. All three men were standing behind podiums and speaking into the microphones. The first question asked by the moderator was a general question that was directed to all three in their respective order. President Bush answered first, and spoke from behind his podium. He stood there talking in a monotone, standing stiffly, like a zombie, never moving and never altering his voice levels. The second person to answer was H. Ross Perot. Taking his cue from the president, he also stood stiff as a board, and spoke in a repetitive, monotonous voice. Next it was Bill Clinton's turn. Much of the country didn't yet know him, who he was, or what he stood for. He was the governor of Arkansas, but had little national recognition. Bill thanked the moderator for the question, then he took the microphone out of its holder and, holding it in his hand, came out from behind the podium and walked to the edge of the stage, right up close to the people. As he spoke, he slowly moved back and forth across the stage, making eye contact with as many people as possible. I don't remember what he was saying, but I turned to my wife and said, "He is going to be our next president." She looked at me with astonished eyes, and asked how I could make such a claim, since no one even knew him. I said, "He knows how to speak."

Bill Clinton went on to win the election, of course, and become the forty-second President of the United States. If he hadn't had the speaking abilities he possessed, would he have won the election? I could never understand why many politicians, and even some celebrities, with all the money and resources at their disposal, never hire someone to teach them how to speak effectively.

Not everyone wants to be a speaker on a stage in an auditorium filled with people. On the other hand, this might be an area that interests you. You might even see yourself as a professional motivational speaker. It is possible, because of the line of work you are in, that you might find yourself onstage giving a lecture of some type. If this happens, some of the suggestions I am offering will help you do a professional job.

Your appearance is very important. You want to look sharp and successful. You want to shine onstage, because hundreds of eyes will be on you. Whether you are a man or a woman, you need to dress with a little bit of flair, but on the conservative side. Remember: this is still business.

Because you are onstage in an auditorium-type atmosphere, your voice alone will probably not carry throughout the room, so you will need to use a microphone. Take a lesson from the Bill Clinton story, and don't stand frozen behind a podium. You can start from there, but don't linger too long. Step out and walk toward your audience. Be animated up there, slowly walking from one end of the stage to the other, holding the microphone in your hand, or better still, around your neck. When you are moving, the eyes of the audience will follow, helping you to keep their attention.

When speaking, look at your audience, make eye contact with various people as you maneuver onstage. Raise or lower your voice when you need to stress points in your presentation. You don't want to be stagnant, speaking in a monotone. Inject a little humor here and there throughout your presentation. Laughter always keeps your audience attentive.

People in the audience came there to learn something or to be inspired. They may have even paid a fee to attend. Don't let them down. Be knowledgeable about your subject, and know how to convey that knowledge to the people who came to hear you. Your goal as the speaker is to have your audience leave the meeting feeling good about themselves, feeling positive about their future, and definitely glad that they came.

Chapter twelve

The Last Chapter

SEVERAL YEARS AGO, I saw a picture that showed a large ship about a block from the pier and heading out to sea. On the side of the ship was its name: *Opportunity.* On the pier was a man in an overcoat, holding a piece of luggage at his side. He looked very sad and disappointed as he stared in the direction of the ship. The caption read, "He missed the boat."

When I first saw that image I was still a young man, but it left an unforgettable lasting impression on me. They say opportunity knocks on everyone's door at least once in his or her life. You have also heard that when opportunity knocks you have to be ready for it. But what if opportunity doesn't knock? Are you going to sit there and wait? Over the years there have been thousands of very successful people to whom opportunity never gave so much as a wink. If you study a cross-section of these people, you will find that many of them didn't sit around and wait. Instead, they took matters into their own hands; they went out and made their own opportunities. The weak wait for opportunities; the strong make them. Use this information to the fullest: go out and make things happen for yourself. Find your own opportunities and run with them.

You are never too young or too old. How many times have you heard someone say, "If only I had done this or done that when I was younger, my life would be different today"? How many times have you heard someone say, "If only I could live my life over again" or "If only I were younger" or "If only I could catch a break"? Life is what you make it. We would all change something in our lives if we could go back, but we can't. We can only go forward, so make the best of the rest of your life. Yesterday is gone, but today IS the first day of the rest of your life. If you ever had a desire to try something that could enrich your life, go for it. Colonel Sanders of Kentucky Fried Chicken fame was a retired sixty-five-year-old trying to make some extra money. His wife fried up a basket of chicken, and he went down the road selling it to people. At age sixty-five, he started an empire. How's that for an accidental goal?

Suddenly There's Money

If you work hard, work smart, and believe in yourself, your payoff will arrive. Sometimes it comes in at a steady pace, and sometimes you hit a payload and suddenly have a lot of money. It's a proven fact that when people who have never had a lot of money suddenly come into large amounts of money, they have no knowledge of to how to handle it. Many spend it so fast that before long they wind up in the same hole they were in when they started.

We have all heard stories of people who have won millions in the lottery only to find themselves broke within two or three years. I have delivered many large life insurance checks to beneficiaries, only to find out later that they blew the money in frivolous ways. You have to control yourself and be sensible and responsible when the money starts to arrive. You have to discipline yourself to spend it wisely. Not only will you be tempted to go on spending sprees, but you will also get bombarded by others who have great ideas on how you can invest it, or have some shaky business schemes, or who simply want you to lend them money. You will also be hearing from numerous charities. You will find that when you are suddenly making money, the word gets out, and everybody comes to you with his or her hands out. Beware of "great ideas," great "investment opportunities," and other wild schemes designed to relieve you of your money.

Startling Facts

Sometime back the Social Security Administration released these startling statistics. Out of every one hundred men who are now twenty-five years of age, here is what happens by the time they are sixty-five:

- **One** will be rich — in fact, wealthy.

- **Four** will have good incomes from collecting rents, investments, etc.

- **Five** will still be working. They would like to retire, but can't afford to because they have to work so they can make ends meet.

- **Thirty-six** will be dead.

- **Fifty-four** will be dependent on relatives, friends, or some sort of charity. These could be older persons living with their children, but without enough income to sustain themselves.

Which category will you find yourself in? I said before that people don't plan to fail — they fail to plan. Certainly all of the one hundred men mentioned above earned money in their life-times. What did they do with it? When I was just starting out in adult life, I read a book that preached saving 10 percent of everything you earn. If you could do this in the forty to forty-five years of your working life, you would be a millionaire-plus by the time you reached retirement age at sixty-five. It isn't always easy to save 10 percent, especially when you are raising a family, but it is easy to save something, even if you start with just $25 or $50 per week and build on that as you move forward. Eighty-five out of one hundred men reaching age sixty-five do not possess as much as $1,000.

Remember: *The difference between an old man and an elderly gentleman is money; likewise, the difference between an old lady and an elderly woman is money.*

How About This for a Plan?

Are you done accumulating money? They say money isn't everything, but today we need it for food, clothing, and other necessities, and we need future money for education, recreation, and retirement. This is where you have to discipline yourself. We all have monthly bills, and the majority of people get those bills paid. Most of us spend a certain amount of money on things that aren't really necessary. Line up all your monthly bills — your electric, gas, phone, rent, groceries, etc. Now set up a new bill. Give your bill your own name; for instance, the "Jones Family Bill." Set it up with a designated amount, and then, every month pay that bill first, into some type of savings program. In other words, pay yourself first, every month. You will find that you'll still have money to pay the other bills. After you do this for two or three months, it will become habit; you won't even notice you are doing it, and you won't miss the money.

People live longer today, which means you will need money for a longer period after retirement. Who is going to give it to you? You will have to do it yourself, and you have to do it on a regular basis, no matter what. Are you doing this now? Here is a test question I want you to answer:

If you save as much money in the next five years as you have already saved in the last five years, how much richer will you be?

The answer might scare you, and the years fly by faster than you think. You are never too young to start saving for tomorrow. Take my advice and do it. You will be glad you did. Look at your age today and count the years left before retirement. Now break those years down into months and then into weeks. How many weeks do you have left to work? How many weeks do you have left to reach your retirement goals? The answer probably is a lot fewer weeks than you thought. Make the best of those weeks. I have followed the advice I'm giving you, and I'm glad I did.

Where Do You Put It?

Everyone has his own ideas on how to save or invest money. I am not attempting to tell you what to do — that's for you to decide. I will simply tell you what I have done and what I believe. I will warn you that I am conservative when it comes to saving and investing my money. I liken myself to the old story of "The Tortoise and the Hare." I never put much money into the stock market because it's too unpredictable for me. You can gain or lose it all in the blink of an eye. If you want to play the stock market, do it with money you can afford to lose. During the economic turndown we are experiencing, many retirees lost their entire retirement savings because their money was in the stock market. It's a terrible thing when people who have worked all their lives, and were depending on their retirement funds to provide for them, suddenly find themselves in their twilight years and broke.

I like investments that are sound and secure, with guarantees to protect me from losing the money I put in — investments such as high-cash-value life insurance policies, annuities, and IRAs opened with a life insurance company. When you use a life insurance company for such vehicles, your money is guaranteed. Also, you are guaranteed a certain minimum interest, regardless of the economy, and when it's time to retire, an insurance company can set you up with a guaranteed income for life, regardless of how old you live to be, and will continue to pay you that income, even if you use up all your initial money. Banks can't do this. I am not suggesting you don't keep any money in a bank, because you need banks also. The money you keep in the bank should be money that you put in and take out as needs arise. The insurance company programs are for the long range. You may hear of other investment vehicles that bring you bigger and faster growth, but those vehicles can also take a dive overnight. If something sounds too good to be true, it probably isn't true. Don't be in a hurry; rather, grow steadily, and most important, solidly. In the long haul you will usually be money ahead. I am the tortoise in that old story. I just keep steadily plugging away, week after week, month after month. I have long since passed the hare.

The Final Review

Now let's review, for the last time, all the points we covered in this book. We started with the meaning of success, and pointed out that true success means more than just having money. To gain the success you want, we stressed keeping a positive attitude and keeping negative thoughts away from your mind. No success can be achieved unless you believe in yourself, believe in your abilities, and believe in the product or service you are providing. You must set goals for yourself, and work systematically toward those goals with a persistence and commitment to get where you are going. Once you decide what your goals are, you must decide that you are going to reach them. You must decide that no one can stop you except yourself, and there is no such thing as "You can't do it."

The next phase of this book took you through the techniques of successful salesmanship, from prospecting to closing the sale. Have you learned from all the various methods we discussed? Some of them are disappearing from the sales world of today, but they are the old standbys, proven methods, and they can help you go above and beyond what most people can imagine. I detailed just what you should expect when you go into business for yourself, both the positives and the negatives, and hopefully gave you the confidence you need when you take that big step of self-employment. Once you are there, it's hard to turn back, because being your own boss can make you feel whole and alive, and show you that there is no limit to what you can achieve and how much money you can make.

Finally I instructed you on how to speak to groups, and deliver your message in a professional and positive way. If you ever find yourself speaking, you will want to look good up there. Next, I am going to discuss prospecting for clients once more, because if you don't prospect, and always look for prospects, chances are you won't succeed.

Everyone Is a Prospect

In chapter 9, "The Arts of Selling," we talked about prospecting for clients, how to prospect, making lists, and cold calling.

I want to revisit the prospecting portion and expand it so you understand that everybody is a prospect. People in my business and in many other businesses involving any type of sales, tend to fall into thinking that a prospect is only someone who falls inside the parameters of their business-related life. When these salespeople go to a store in the evening, take a holiday, or whenever they are not actively working at their business, some quit thinking about making sales, even though they are meeting and talking with people regularly. If you truly want success, you have to be thinking sales at all times. You have to eat, breathe, and sleep sales, and you have to always remember that everybody is a prospect.

I offer you these next few examples from my own experience. In 1972, my first wife and I divorced. Divorce was not my area of expertise, and I was ignorant of what to expect. It probably didn't make a difference anyway, because in 1972, there was no such thing as "men's rights." I chose not to hire my own attorney, but instead used hers, thinking he would be fair and just. Well, as you might expect, I lost my home and pretty much everything else, but I got even with that lawyer. Two weeks after the divorce was final, I sold him life insurance.

As the regional vice president for the Decatur Company, I found myself on the Illinois Tollway almost every day. When traveling the tollway, I always paid the tolls at a tollbooth manned by a person, so I could get a receipt, which is tax deductible if it's business travel. One particular tollbooth always had the same attendant. After a couple of weeks we got to say hello to each other, and then talk when possible, and you guessed it — before long, he and his wife purchased life insurance policies from me.

A few years back, my wife, Catherine, and I took a train trip to Tucson, Arizona. We rented a room in a sleeper car. Each sleeper car has an exclusive attendant who is there to serve and pamper you. The trip between Chicago and Tucson netted me two life insurance policies from the attendant.

In my business at the insurance agency, I deal with several different companies for different insurance products. Each of these companies has what is called a field representative, a person who spends his or her entire day calling on insurance agents. Field reps don't usually sell insurance, but they still need it themselves. They see hundreds of insurance agents all year long, and none of these agents asks them about their own insurance needs, except me. I insure five field representatives from five different companies.

This last example involves a stockbroker. One of the life insurance companies I represent is publicly traded, and I own stock in it. The company uses one particular stockbroker to make a market in their stock. The company has over 1,000 agents, many of whom have used the broker to purchase stock. No one ever asked him if he needed insurance, except me. Because I asked, he purchased life insurance from me.

I didn't write the preceding to brag about my accomplishments, but rather to drive home the fact that everybody is a prospect. You have to be thinking at all times, and asking everyone you meet, because regardless of what product or service you are offering, it's a good bet that everyone can use it.

The Pep Talk You Have Been Waiting For

I have explained as many selling techniques as I thought necessary, tried to teach you how to use these techniques, and threw in some of my own experiences. It wouldn't be fitting to close the book without giving you a pep talk.

I have come across many salespersons who believed, incorrectly, that the only sales worth pursuing were the big ones. They let the little sales slip right through their fingers. In the course of building my business, I have never felt that way. I want every sale I can get, large or small, because my purpose is to build and service the customers. You build a house one brick at a time; you don't wait for a wall to be delivered. Go after every sale, even the small ones, because the small ones will lead you to the larger ones. *Great opportunities come to those who make the most of small ones.* I can't tell you how many times I made a small sale that led me to a very large one. You want them all. The person who waits for the large sale, and lets all of the small ones go by, usually doesn't get the large sale he has been waiting for, and then he has nowhere else to go.

When you are out there dealing with people, always let them think you are busy. Always let them think you are successful, because people want to deal with successful people. Never use high pressure, but be persistent and professional. Always give your people the personal touch, because people like it, and it makes them feel special.

We have all heard the saying "A mind is a terrible thing to waste." I am going to go a step further and say to you, "A dream is a terrible thing to waste." If you have a dream, go for it. If you don't try, you will always wish and wonder what could have been. You will be unhappy, and may even come to resent your life. Dreams can motivate you, and dreams can come true. Dreams can make you successful. Don't sit back and look at your life and wonder what happened. Get up, get out, give it a try, and make things happen. Don't burn your bridges until you feel secure, but for sure burn them. Don't let anyone tell you that you can't do it. Don't let anyone tell you how to work or what to do for a living. It's your life. Live it to your fullest, and enjoy it as much as you can. Work at what you like to do, and it won't feel like work at all. If you believe in yourself, don't let yourself down. Don't sit there thinking about bettering your life. Make a decision today, and do something about it.

Remember, we all put our pants on the same way. I am not super-rich, but I have made a good living, and have accomplished things that I am proud of. I don't think I am anybody special. I simply took the knowledge I gained, starting with the Decatur School, and the knowledge I learned through experience, and ran with it to make the best of my life that I could. If I could do it over again, I wouldn't change a thing, because I am happy and am where I want to be. Are you where you want to be? If your answer is no, I encourage you to begin planning where you want to be immediately, set your sights on your goal, and then GO FOR IT!

About the Author

JOHN J. TASSONE was born and raised in Chicago. As a child, he had a newspaper route, shined shoes, and made deliveries for a meat market. Throughout high school he worked in his father's hardware store. He earned a bachelor's degree in Education at Chicago Teachers College (now Chicago State University), then taught drafting in the Chicago public school system, after which he taught drafting to inmates at the Chicago House of Corrections. He then worked as a design draftsman for U.S. Steel, during which time he also moonlighted at two other jobs.

While working at U.S. Steel, John started selling life insurance part-time in September 1967. After a year, he quit U.S. Steel to go full-time. He moved up through the insurance company ranks quickly, and became regional VP of the Chicago area. In 1976, he opened his own agency, Associated General Insurance Agency of Illinois. John and his wife, Catherine, live near Chicago.